Konrad Gesner

OUTWARD BOUND

OUTWARD BOUND

BY

SUTTON VANE

BONI AND LIVERIGHT
PUBLISHERS :: :: NEW YORK

CAUTION

ALL dramatic rights for Sutton Vane's *Outward Bound* in North America are owned and controlled by William Harris, Jr., Hudson Theatre, New York City. Special notice should be taken that possession of this book without a valid contract for production first having been obtained from Mr. Harris confers no right or license to professionals or amateurs to produce the play publicly or in private for gain or charity. Until further notice performances of this play in North America will be limited to those companies which appear under Mr. Harris's direction, and he absolutely forbids other performances by professionals or amateurs, including "readings," tableaux, and anything of such nature approximating a performance. The play is fully protected by copyright and any violations will be prosecuted.

ACT OF MARCH 4, 1909: SECTION 28

"That any person who wilfully or for profit shall infringe any copyright secured by this act, or who shall knowingly and wilfully aid or abet such infringement shall be deemed guilty of a misdemeanor, and upon conviction thereof shall be punished by imprisonment for not exceeding one year, or by a fine of not less than $100 nor more than $1000, or both, in the discretion of the Court."

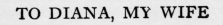

TO DIANA, MY WIFE

CHARACTERS

(In order of their appearance)

SCRUBBY *Chow*
ANN *my*
HENRY *Luke Yates*
MR. PRIOR *teacher*
MRS. CLIVEDEN-BANKS *Bob Defenbaher*
REV. WILLIAM DUKE *Irene Rhue*
MRS. MIDGET *Walt, Thyyasson*
MR. LINGLEY
REV. FRANK THOMSON *School*

Scene: On board ship.
Time: The present.

ACT I

In harbour.   Morning.

ACT II

At sea.   The same evening.

ACT III

About six days later.

Scene I.   Afternoon.
Scene II.   The night of the same day.

"OUTWARD BOUND" *was first produced at the Everyman Theatre, Hampstead, London, on Monday, the 17th of September, 1923, with the following cast:*

SCRUBBY	STANLEY LATHBURY
ANN	DIANA HAMILTON
HENRY	WILLIAM STACK
MR. PRIOR	FREDERICK COOPER
MRS. CLIVEDEN-BANKS .	GLADYS FFOLLIOTT
REV. WILLIAM DUKE . .	FREDERICK LEISTER
MRS. MIDGET	CLARE GREET
MR. LINGLEY	ARTHUR PAGE
REV. FRANK THOMSON .	ROY BYFORD

"OUTWARD BOUND" *was first presented in America by William Harris, Jr., at the Apollo Theatre, Atlantic City, N. J., on Monday, the 24th of December, 1923, with the following cast:*

SCRUBBY	J. M. KERRIGAN
ANN	MARGALO GILLMORE
HENRY	LESLIE HOWARD
MR. PRIOR	ALFRED LUNT
MRS. CLIVEDEN-BANKS .	CHARLOTTE GRAN-VILLE
REV. WILLIAM DUKE . .	LYONEL WATTS
MRS. MIDGET	BERYL MERCER
MR. LINGLEY	EUGENE POWERS
REV. FRANK THOMSON .	DUDLEY DIGGES

Under the stage direction of Robert Milton; the scenery by Livingston Platt.

ACT I

ACT I

ACT I

The curtain rises on a room which suggests rather than represents the lounge smoke-room of a small ocean liner. There is a bar on the right with the usual array of glasses and bottles on the counter and on the shelves behind it. On the extreme left is a small writing table, and the rest of the furniture consists of the usual small round tables and swivel arm-chairs that are found in the smoke-room on most liners. Around the room at the back is a red cushioned wall-seat. The carpet is of warm neutral tone. There are three doors: one behind the bar, another leading off left and a third, centre, opening on to the deck. This centre door is wide open, and behind it can be seen the liner railings. The colour of the sky at the back arrests the attention at once. It is a curious colour—vague and almost nondescript. There are four portholes in the back wall, fitted up with small curtains which are now drawn. Three large lights hang from the ceiling, and some small lamp brackets on the walls. The sun is shining, and it is a clear still morning. Behind the bar stands SCRUBBY, *busy polishing the glasses—preparatory to the boat sailing. He is dressed in the usual uniform of a ship's steward. His manner is always calm and reposeful, and his voice gentle and kindly. He is an elderly man, typically English.*

ANN is seen to pass along the deck, and she comes through the centre door into the room. She is wearing a hat and coat, underneath which is a simple but very smart clinging frock of green. She is young, but one sees at once that she is terribly nervous. She pauses and looks round in a frightened manner. Then SCRUBBY clinks a glass and she turns and sees him.

ANN. Oh, I beg your pardon—good morning.

SCRUBBY. Good morning, madam.

ANN. I'm sorry to bother you, but I'm afraid we've lost our way.

SCRUBBY. Where do you want to get to, madam?

ANN. The cabins, of course.

SCRUBBY. Cabins?

ANN. Yes! Where we sleep. I'm afraid I'm awfully stupid. I've never been on the sea before.

SCRUBBY. The old ship will be highly flattered. You'll find all the berths right forward (*points to the left*) down there.

[16]

ANN. Thank you very much. (*She goes up to the centre and speaks to someone outside.*) Henry, come along, dear, I was quite right, this is the way. (HENRY *enters from the deck. He is wearing a well-cut lounge suit and a dark soft hat. He is an ardent young man, about thirty years old. He is good looking, quietly emotional, serious and sincere. He is rather mystic in manner, and behaves like a dazed man who has recently received a severe shock.*)

HENRY. Sorry, I was looking at the sea. What did you say?

ANN. This *is* the way, dear.

HENRY. Oh, good! We'll probably find all our stuff in the cabin already. How did you find out?

ANN. *He* told me. (*Indicating* SCRUBBY.)

HENRY. Oh!—good morning!

SCRUBBY. Good morning, sir.

(ANN *moves down to left.*)

HENRY. Bit confusing these boats, aren't they?

SCRUBBY. Yes, sir, to begin with.

ANN. Come along, dear.

HENRY. I say, I'm feeling awfully tired.

ANN. Do you wonder?—after what you've been through?

[17]

HENRY. No, I suppose I don't. I can't quite focus it all even now, you know. By Jove, we'll have a gorgeous trip though, won't we?

ANN. Yes, dear.

HENRY. The rest—the peace and—and—

ANN. Don't worry so, dear.

HENRY. And the forgetfulness—

ANN. Of course, dear, don't worry.

HENRY. No, I won't, I won't! (*To* SCRUBBY.) Thanks for telling my—my wife the way.

ANN. Give me your hand.

HENRY. What's that?

ANN. Give me your hand, dear.

HENRY. Oh! You treat me like a child! I'm quite all right really.

ANN. Give me your hand. (*He goes to her, takes her hand.*) There!

HENRY. Thanks for the hand.

ANN. Come along.

(*They go off together, left, and a moment later* TOM PRIOR *enters by the centre door.* PRIOR *is a slight young man, highly strung. He is not specifically drunk at the moment, but rather more displays the mellow and bland cock-sureness of a youth who for some time has kept himself going with constant stimulants. He is wearing a lounge suit, and is very cheerful and smiling.)*

Tom. Oh!—er—good morning, steward.

Scrubby. Good morning, sir.

Tom. This is the smoke-room, I suppose?

Scrubby. Yes, sir.

Tom. Look here, then—er—how long before we sail?

Scrubby. About a quarter of an hour—sir—or more—or less.

Tom. Then I say, could I—er—I get a drink?

Scrubby. Certainly, sir.

Tom. Bravo! (*He crosses to the bar.*) I want it.

Scrubby. What shall I get you, sir?

Tom. A Scotch.

Scrubby. Any soda-water, sir?

Tom. No, thank you.

Scrubby. All Scotch!

[19]

Tom.   As a matter of fact, steward, you'll probably see a lot of me during this trip.   Yes, you'll
get to know me quite well, so I thought I'd warn you
to begin with.

Scrubby.   (*Serves drink.*)   The warning is an
honour, sir.

Tom.   Yes, thanks.   How much is it?

Scrubby.   Oh, you needn't pay, sir.

Tom.   What!

Scrubby.   If you'll just sign this.   (*Presents chit
book.*)

Tom.   Oh yes, of course, I'd forgotten that catch.
(*Bus.*)   Have one yourself?

Scrubby.   No thank you, sir.

Tom.   (*Drinks.*)   Ah, that's better.   As a matter
of fact, steward, I'd a rather thick night last night—

Scrubby.   Indeed, sir.

Tom.   Yes—yes—and I want pulling together.
By Jove—it must have been a jolly thick night because I can't remember anything about it now.   But
never mind.   (*Drinks again.*)   It's a gorgeous morning, anyway.

Scrubby.   It is, sir.   A pity some people should
be alive to spoil it.

TOM.   What's that?

SCRUBBY.   I was talking to myself, sir.

TOM.   I say, steward, how many passengers have we got?

SCRUBBY.   Not many, sir, it's our slack time of year.

TOM.   The last time I came out—why—it must be over ten years ago—I was going tea planting, and —and—I was only about nineteen—and— (*Pause.*) Phew, how time flies! Get me some cigarettes.

SCRUBBY.   Yes, sir! Egyptians, Turkish or Virginian?

TOM.   Gold Flake.   What's the old Captain like?

SCRUBBY.   Very decent sort I've heard say, sir. Very respected, I *know.*

TOM.   Oh, I don't like that sort—not on these small ships.   Now when I went out before—

SCRUBBY.   Your cigarettes, sir

TOM.   Thank you.   And get me another drink. The same.

(MRS. CLIVEDEN-BANKS *enters from the centre and goes down to* TOM.   *She is a withered old harridan of fifty odd—probably once beautiful.   Smartly frocked in travelling costume.   She carries an armful of magazines.*)

[21]

Mrs. C-Banks. Aha! I thought I knew that voice!

Tom. What! (*Rises, turns.*) Oh, really! Good gracious! Mrs. Cliveden-Banks! How are you? What a surprise! (*Shakes hands.*)

Mrs. C-Banks. I saw your name on the passenger list, so I asked for the bar at once, and here you are! (*Sits left of table.*)

Tom. Delighted. Come and sit down. What are you doing here? (*Sits above table.*)

Mrs. C-Banks. Joining my dear husband. And I'm afraid we're in for a very dull trip. There is nobody on board—at least nobody who *is* anybody. Though, of course, the poor creatures can't help that. You follow me. What I say I mean in the most kindly manner—but still, there it is.

Tom. We must try and cheer each other up, then, Mrs. Banks.

Mrs. C-Banks. Yes, all friends at sea, of course. By the way, my name is *Cliveden*-Banks. You know, of course, but it's such a long while since we met. There was a plain Mrs. Banks in the divorce court lately—so silly of her—and so plain, judging from the Daily Mirror—a total stranger, of course. Still it's made me very particular about my hyphen. Not that I am ever likely to appear in a divorce court.

Tom. No, most unlikely. (*With a significant appraisal of her.*)

Mrs. C-Banks. Still you see what I mean.

(Scrubby *puts drink on table.*)

Tom. Of course. Thank you. Mrs. *Cliveden*-Banks, will you have a drink?

Mrs. C-Banks. Thank you—what are you drinking—ginger ale?

Tom. No—er—whiskey.

Mrs. C-Banks. At this time in the morning?

Tom. Whiskey at any time in the morning, afternoon or evening.

Mrs. C-Banks. I'm afraid you're still a naughty boy. I'll have a ginger ale. (Scrubby *proceeds to fetch her the drink.*) When I said there was nobody on board, dear Mr. Prior, between you and me, there is one person on board to whom I shall take a strong objection. He's a clergyman.

Tom. Poor blighter! I should pity rather than blame him.

Mrs. C-Banks. Oh, don't you know? Clergymen at sea are dreadfully unlucky. We shall probably all go to the bottom. If we do I shall blame the clergyman entirely. In my opinion steamship

companies have no right to let clergymen travel at
all. The clergy ought to stay at home in their own
parishes and do good, not go gadding about all over
the world putting other people's lives in danger.

Scrubby. Your ginger ale, madam! (*Puts drink
on table.*)

Mrs. C-Banks. Thank you, steward. (*Takes
drink.*) Isn't that so?

Scrubby. Isn't what so, madam?

Mrs. C-Banks. Oh, you must have been listening to what I was saying.

Scrubby. I assure you, madam, I was not.

Mrs. C-Banks. How odd! (Tom *signs for
drink.*) I was remarking that the sea-faring men
regard the presence of a clergyman on board your
ship as highly unlucky.

Scrubby. I believe there is a superstition to that
effect, madam, yes. (*Returns behind bar.*)

Mrs. C-Banks. There! I told you so. Well,
the best thing we can do is to cut the fellow dead.
Nicely, of course, but firmly.

Tom. Just as you like. But will we save the
boat by doing it?

Mrs. C-Banks. How droll you are!

[24]

TOM.   Look out! Talk of the—

(THE REV. WILLIAM DUKE *enters left, crosses to desk and looks for writing paper and envelope. As he does so he speaks to* TOM. DUKE *is a very sincere, earnest young clergyman.*)

DUKE.   Good morning, sir

TOM.   (*In a loud voice to* MRS. C-BANKS.)   How is the Colonel?

MRS. C-BANKS. Dear. Benjamin, I regret to say, is feeling the heat dreadfully. I should have joined him last year, but somehow I never got time. The penalty of popularity. My great friend, Mabel, the Duchess of Middleford—*you don't* know her, of course, she was only saying to me at the Palace the other day—

DUKE.   (*As he sits at writing desk with paper, etc., turns to* TOM.)   Good morning.

TOM.   Eh—oh, good morning.

MRS. C-BANKS.   Who is that man?

TOM.   Really, Mrs. Cliveden-Banks, I dunno— I—

MRS. C-BANKS. How strange! Peculiar people one must meet, mustn't one, in public places? Never mind. Let me see, where was I?

Tom. With your great friend whom I don't know.

Mrs. C-Banks. Oh, yes, of course. (Rev. William Duke *sits left and writes.*) And then that strange man whom we neither of us know interrupted by wishing you good morning. Never mind. Mabel pointed out to me very clearly that I was in danger of neglecting my duty. She said to me quite plainly, almost brutally, and she can be very brutal sometimes—"My dear Genevieve," she said, "you must remember you are a daughter of the Empire, a soldier's *daughter*—a soldier's *wife*. Your place is by your husband's side in far, far India." In fact she was so insistent on my leaving England that if I didn't know her really well, I should have felt she wanted to get rid of me. Still I have taken her advice, I have abandoned London's gaieties and go to help poor dear Benjamin rule a lot of black men. Frankly I hate the idea.

Duke. (*Still sitting at table, turns.*) I'm awfully sorry to bother you, madam, but could you tell me what the date is?

Mrs. C-Banks. What was that?

Duke. I ought to know, of course, seeing that it's the date we sail, but my memory's so—

Mrs. C-Banks. Did you say the date?

[26]

DUKE. Yes, if you please.

MRS. C-BANKS. The *date?*

DUKE. If you would—

MRS. C-BANKS. You're trying to start a conversation with me, aren't you?

DUKE. (*Laughs.*) Well, frankly, as we're all to be shipmates, the sooner we get to know each other the better, don't you think?

MRS. C-BANKS. That, young man, is a matter of opinion.

DUKE. Oh, I'm awfully sorry if—I didn't think introductions were necessary on board ship.

MRS. C-BANKS. Possibly they may not have been in the days of Walter Raleigh. Not having been there myself at the time, I cannot say for certain. But customs change at sea, young man, even though the Church remains exactly where it always was. Under the circumstances, therefore, there can be no question of me giving you a date.

DUKE. I beg your pardon—I'll find it out for myself.

MRS. C-BANKS. Was that cutting enough, dear Mr. Prior?

TOM. Oh yes, most; but what did it mean?

Mrs. C-Banks.　I don't know.

(Mrs. Midget *wanders on from the deck. A poor charwoman in black little bonnet, black shawl and dress—her best. Very humble, simple and obviously out of place in these strange surroundings. But sweet and motherly.*)

Mrs. Midget.　You'll excuse me, mum, but—

Mrs. C-Banks.　(*Looking up and seeing her.*) Good gracious!

Mrs. Midget.　You'll excuse me speaking up as it were, but I must say something to someone. And as you're the only other lady I've seen about, bar myself, I must ask you to give me a—

Mrs. C-Banks.　Mr. Prior, am I to be attacked from all sides?

Mrs. Midget. (*Starts suddenly on hearing name.*)　Mr. Prior?

Tom.　Any objection?

Mrs. Midget.　No, very pleased to meet you. You see, mum, I 'ad to follow yer because yer see, mum, I've been struck all of a 'eap.

Mrs. C-Banks.　You've been what?

Mrs. Midget.　Struck all of a 'eap.

[28]

MRS. C-BANKS. Mr. Prior, rescue me. And you had better do something for this good woman, too. It appears she has been struck all of a heap—whatever that may mean.

TOM. Well—what's the trouble?

MRS. MIDGET. Well, sir, thanking you, it's like this, as it were—

MRS. C-BANKS. "As it were." How quaint! "As it was" is correct, of course—we all know that from our Prayer Book. Go on.

MRS. MIDGET. Well, sir, it were like this, *as it was;* only last Saturday, Mrs. Roberts and I were talking about the sheets being damp, and I says—

MRS. C-BANKS. Ah! Sheets—damp. The good woman is, of course, a stewardess.

TOM. Are you?

MRS. MIDGET. Am I what?

TOM. A stewardess on this boat?

MRS. MIDGET. No, I'm a passenger.

MRS. C-BANKS. She's a passenger! Oh, I see it, she's a passenger! I see it all! The whole thing has come to me in a flash! She's a passenger. Don't worry yourself any more, Mr. Prior, I have solved the good woman's trouble. She's a passenger and she's lost her way; haven't you, good woman?

MRS. MIDGET. Exactly, mum.

MRS. C-BANKS. Mr. Prior, tell that steward fellow to tell somebody to take the good woman back to her proper place immediately. She's been wandering. She's on the wrong deck, she's in the wrong class. Goodbye, good woman, goodbye. So glad to have been so helpful.

MRS. MIDGET. Thank you, mum.

TOM. (*Going to her.*) Oh, steward, just get someone to show this woman steerage—er—third class deck—or something, will you?

SCRUBBY. (*Turns to* TOM.) The third class, sir?

TOM. Yes, please.

SCRUBBY. I think you've made some mistake, sir. There is only one class on the boat.

(REV. WILLIAM DUKE *finishes his letter and goes out left.*)

MRS. C-BANKS. (*Faintly.*) What was that?

TOM. Only one class?

SCRUBBY. Yes, sir. It's the same on all this line.

Mrs. C-Banks.   What was that?

Tom.   Oh, sorry—I didn't know.   (*Returning.*)
Er—Mrs. Cliveden-Banks—

Mrs. C-Banks.   Mr. Prior, did I, or did I not
hear that fellow say there is only one class on this
boat?

Tom.   He said so, certainly.

Mrs. C-Banks.   Mr. Prior, the thing's impossible.

Tom.   Well, he ought to know.

Mrs. C-Banks.   How dare she—how dare my
secretary book me a passage on a vessel with only
one class?   How am I to know who are the ladies
and gentlemen, and who are not?

Tom.   Now, now, don't get excited.

Mrs. C-Banks.   Excited!   Mr. Prior, a terrible
thought has struck me.   That woman there—

Tom.   Well, what about her?

Mrs. C-Banks.   She probably eats.

Tom.   Extremely likely, I should say.

Mrs. C-Banks.   Well then—if she eats—and if
there's only one class—she will eat in the same place

as we shall.   It can't be done, I shall disembark immediately.

Tom.   Now look here, Mrs. Banks—Mrs. Cliveden-Banks—she's probably only a lady's maid or something.

Mrs. C-Banks.   Who would have a maid like that—outside a theatrical boarding house?

Tom.   The idea of your landing is absurd.   Don't get nervy about nothing.   We can easily avoid her. If you're really upset—

Mrs. C.-Banks.   And I am, I am!

Tom.   Then I'll question her.

Mrs. C-Banks.   Yes.   Do, do, quickly.   It would be quite impossible for me to lunch at the same table with a woman who has been struck all of a heap.

Tom.   Come here, will you?   I—er—we want to help you if we possibly can.   (*Drinks.*)

Mrs. Midget.   Thank you, sir.

Tom.   Excuse me.   (*Finishes drink.*)   Thanks. Now, what is—your name?

Mrs. Midget.   Midget.

Tom.   What?

Mrs. Midget.   Midget.

Mrs. C-Banks. That, to begin with, is an alibi. No one could possibly be called Midget.

Mrs. Midget. (*Warming in quick resentment.*) Oh, couldn't they? Well, I'll show you whether they could or not all right. Midget's as good a name as any other name, Midget is. And don't you forget it, old Mrs. 'Igh and Mighty. My name's Midget all right, Midget married me all right, and I can prove it, and I've got my lines, which was a job to get as I admit.

Mrs. C-Banks. How dreadfully sordid!

Mrs. Midget. But when it comes to utter strangers tellin' me as I don't know what my own name is, then I speaks up and unabashed, as I would do in front of the 'ole street. I've nothing to 'ide, I've not, I'm not one of these—

Mrs. C-Banks. That will do, that will do. The world is full of troubles, we know. Doubtless you have had yours, my good—er—my woman.

Mrs. Midget. I 'ave 'ad trouble, I confess.

Tom. But what's your present one—that's what—what we want to know?

Mrs. Midget. Where am I?

Tom. On board—on board this ship.

Mrs. Midget. Yes, but what for?

[33]

Tom. How should *I* know? Are your tickets and luggage all right?

Mrs. Midget. I suppose so. I'm not one to worry over little things.

Tom. Have you been to your cabin yet?

Mrs. Midget. No.

Tom. What's the number?

Mrs. Midget. 'Ow do I know if I ain't been there?

Tom. I say—you're not tight, are you?

Mrs. Midget. Tight?

Tom. Blotto—squiffy—gone away.

Mrs. Midget. Not me. "To. T.," I am.

Tom. How wise of you. (*Drinks.*) Well, are you ill?

Mrs. Midget. Now, that's what I'm a-wondering. Am I ill? I don't think so. I don't feel ill. And yet I said to Mrs. Roberts last Thursday—or was it Wednesday?—never mind, I said to 'er anyway I says—"What I want" says I—or did she say it to me? Never mind, it don't make no difference, one of us says to the other, "What I or you want," according to whichever of us *did* say it, "is a thorough 'oliday." And then—wait a minute—I

[34]

remember now—it's all coming back—I've come on 'ere to meet somebody.

TOM. Oh, that's it, is it?

MRS. MIDGET. Yes, at the other end. It was our parson's idea. "A thorough 'oliday" of course! 'Ow silly of me to forget. But of course I ain't 'ad much to eat to-day and what with the excitement and one thing and another, and Mrs. Roberts—

TOM. Damn Mrs. Roberts!

MRS. MIDGET. Oh, I do, sir—often.

TOM. Look here, what you want's a sandwich and a drink, and a good sleep. Then you'll remember everything. Someone should have brought you here, of course. But if you're being met at the other end, there's nothing to worry about.

MRS. MIDGET. Thank you, sir.

MRS. C-BANKS. The woman is obviously light-headed. Have her removed.

TOM. Steward, can you find out this passenger's stewardess for me—for her? Have her put in her charge, see she gets everything she should have. Nervous you know, never been to sea.

SCRUBBY. Certainly, sir. (*Crosses left from behind bar.*)

[35]

Mrs. C-Banks. I should certainly suggest a sleep for her. A long, long sleep—in fact, if I were in her place I should take a complete rest, have all my meals in my own cabin, and never come on deck at all. I'm sure she would feel better if she did that.

Mrs. Midget. Much obliged. But I 'ope to be 'opping about like a cricket in an 'our or two.

Scrubby. This way, madam.

Mrs. Midget. (*Flattered by the attention.*) Thank you, *Captain.*

(Scrubby *and* Mrs. Midget *go off together left.*)

Scrubby. Straight ahead.

Mrs. C-Banks. I should like to burn Miss Longton. Miss Longton is my secretary.

Tom. (*Looking after them.*) Do you think that woman was speaking the truth?

Mrs. C-Banks. No. She's probably one of a gang of international crooks. Look at the way she scraped acquaintance with me. Personally I shall be on my guard against her. (*Low muffled siren heard.*) What do you think that is?

Tom   Sailing shortly, I suppose.

MRS. C-BANKS. Then I shall go on deck and wave farewell to the dear old white cliffs. (*Rises.*) By the way, I'm told on many parts of the coast they're crumbling fast. Still, England, England, there is no country like her.

TOM. Thank goodness.

MRS. C-BANKS. Why do you say that?

TOM. I don't. That's what other countries say.

MRS. C-BANKS. How naughty you are. Well, come along and protect me from the mob.

TOM. No, thanks, if you'll excuse me. I'd far rather remain here and slip away from my native land oblivious of her disregard for me.

MRS. C-BANKS. Which means—?

TOM. That I'm going to have another drink.

MRS. C-BANKS. You're a bad lad. Still, I'll see you later.

(*She passes through the centre door and goes left along the deck.*)

TOM. I suppose so. Confound the woman. (*Drinks and lights cigarette.*)

(REV. WILLIAM DUKE *re-appears from the left.*)

Oh, I say, Padre!

DUKE.   How is the Colonel?

TOM.   Padre.

DUKE.   Were you speaking to me, sir?

TOM.   Yes.   I want to—to apologise.

DUKE.   (*Centre.*)   What for?

TOM.   Cutting you stone dead like the silly old woman I was with.

DUKE.   Oh, that's all right.

TOM.   Sure?

DUKE.   Sure!

TOM.   Positive?

DUKE.   Positive!

TOM.   Good.   Have a drink?   (*Leading him to bar.*)

DUKE.   Thanks.

TOM.   The fellow will be back in a second.

DUKE.   Good.

TOM.   Cigarette?

DUKE.   Thanks.

TOM.   Hot, isn't it?

DUKE. Yes. Hot.

TOM. Yes—er—do you think we shall have—er—smooth passage?

DUKE. Quite. I mean—I hope so.

TOM. So do I.

DUKE. I suppose we all do.

TOM. Er—yes. I suppose we all do. I say, I must tell you, of course, that I should never have behaved as I did just now, pretending not to see you and all that, but of course I'm a very weak character.

DUKE. Strong of you to admit it.

TOM. Yes, I'm easily swayed. No stamina. (*Drinks.*) I can't think why. And the old cat was drivelling along, and she persuaded me not to see you. Told me you were unlucky.

DUKE. Ha!

TOM. So I agreed not to. I always agree with anyone I'm with. She was to blame entirely.

DUKE. I have always found it an unwise habit to run down other people. They have a nasty way of getting to hear about it and retaliating—with interest.

TOM. You're not going to preach a sermon, are you?

Duke. Good Lor', no! I say, do you know the slums?

Tom.   Good heavens, no!

Duke.   Take my advice then and don't; I do. I've known them for the last eight years. And I'm sick of the slums and people I was trying to keep straight with sermons—official and otherwise—and the drizzle, and the smell of tea in urns with the Vicar—oh yes, the Vicar more than anything. No, no, no more sermons from me for a bit. But I beg your pardon, I must be boring you.

Tom.   Not at all so far. You must have had a pretty rotten time!

(Scrubby *re-enters from the left and goes to bar*.)

Duke.   Oh, I don't know, I'm awfully keen on my job. I want a rest, that's all.

Tom.   "A thorough 'oliday," in fact.   Hello, here's our man. This will do you good. What's it to be?

Duke.   Beer, please.

Tom.   Er—steward—er—what *is* your name?

Scrubby.   Scrubby.

Tom.   Midget and Scrubby. Good Lor'! Oh, well, it can't be helped, I suppose. A Bass please, and a—the same.

[40]

TOM. Oh yes, of course. That lady. Thanks very much.

SCRUBBY. Thank you, sir.

DUKE. I say, I really oughtn't to know, but I'd always understood you couldn't get a drink on board a ship until she sailed?

TOM. Neither you can as a rule. That never struck me—don't say anything.

DUKE. It's very queer.

TOM. It's very lucky. Cheero!

DUKE. Cheero!

TOM. Got any other gadget on you for the passengers' amusement? Perhaps you'd like me to walk the plank or something?

DUKE. We ought to have some sports, of course.

TOM. Why did I put the idea into your head?

DUKE. You can help with the organisation. You need not participate.

TOM. Right. I'll organise anything you like— from here. Cheery spot this.

(*Through the centre door enters* MR. LINGLEY. *He is a hard and unpleasant business man, aged fifty-*

five or sixty. He is loud and officious, and is obviously self-made. He has on a travelling cap and a heavy overcoat, and he is carrying an attaché case, containing business papers. He is evidently in a great hurry.)

LINGLEY. Ah, good morning, gentlemen. My name's Lingley.

TOM. Hurray!

LINGLEY. I've had a narrow shave—nearly missed her.

DUKE. Duke's my name. Very warm to-day, sir.

LINGLEY. Damn warm—I beg your pardon, I didn't notice your collar—very warm. Steward, get me a drink. (*Sits at table left.*)

SCRUBBY. Whiskey and soda, sir?

LINGLEY. No, confound you, ginger ale with some ice. Yes, I left it a bit too late, another five minutes and I'd have missed her.

DUKE. We'll soon be off then?

LINGLEY. We're sailing now.

TOM. Land of hope and glory—au revoir! (*Drinks.*)

DUKE.   You motored here?

LINGLEY.   No, flew—in my office two hours ago.   Now I must get on with things.   (*Opens attaché case and lays out papers.*)

(SCRUBBY *brings him his drink.*)

DUKE.   (*To* TOM.)   There you are, you see, the man's keen.

TOM.   I *know* the blighter.

LINGLEY.   (*To* SCRUBBY.)   How much?

SCRUBBY.   You needn't pay, sir.

LINGLEY.   I always pay.   How much?

SCRUBBY.   One shilling, sir.

LINGLEY.   Damn—er—*very* expensive still—here is *one* shilling.

SCRUBBY.   Thank you, sir.

LINGLEY.   What for?   (SCRUBBY *returns behind bar.*)   I haven't tipped you.

DUKE.   I hope you won't be so busy, sir, that we shan't see you on the trip.

LINGLEY.   Once in my state-room I don't suppose I'll leave it—till we touch—er—er—Marseilles.

DUKE.   I hope it's interesting work, sir.

[45]

LINGLEY.   No, it isn't, but it keeps me busy—
I am an M.P. you know.

(SCRUBBY *disappears through the door right.*)

DUKE.   Oh!   Pleased to meet you.

LINGLEY.   Not at all.   I'm on the London
County Council as well, incidentally I own twenty-
one music-halls, a chain of cinemas, two gold mines
and a Methodist chapel.   Naturally they want looking after.

DUKE.   Naturally.   What are you doing with the
chapel?

LINGLEY.   Having it pulled down.

TOM.   Sportsman!

LINGLEY.   You—you there!

TOM.   Me?

LINGLEY.   Yes!   I know your face, don't I?
I never forget a face.

TOM.   How that must sadden your sweet life at
times.

LINGLEY.   Where have I seen it before?

TOM.   Oh, in your office.   You gave me a job
once.   It lasted two days.

LINGLEY.   What was the matter?

[46]

TOM. Your office! I couldn't stand the atmosphere, so I drowned it in drink.

LINGLEY. I remember. I remember. You were sacked mechanically.

TOM. Yes. You wouldn't give me a second chance.

LINGLEY. No one has ever given *me* a second chance. I shall never expect one. I shall certainly never ask for one.

TOM. As you said when you sacked me mechanically. In my opinion, Mr. Lingley, L.C.C., M.P., you're a pompous old idiot.

LINGLEY. (*Rising.*) How dare you! How— you must be crazy.

TOM. I'm not in your ghastly office now. I can say what I like. (*Shouts.*) You're a blue-nosed baboon! There! I've dreamt I said that to you for weeks, and now I've said it.

LINGLEY. If you're not careful, Mr.—Mr.—er— er—I'll—I'll—

TOM. If *you're* not careful, Mr. Lingley, I'll make you walk the plank at the sports.

LINGLEY. Mr. Prior, you are obviously drunk now.

TOM. I am drunk, I admit—but I had trusted not obviously.

DUKE. Dear, dear, dear, dear!

TOM. Yes, that remark helps matters such a lot, doesn't it?

LINGLEY. I shall go on deck. Where are my papers? I've been irritated. The doctors said I must not be irritated. I've too much to do to be irritated.

DUKE. Oh, I'm sure Mr. Prior didn't mean—

TOM. I did. Every word of it. Shut up! He's a pink-eyed rabbit. He's a rotter, he's a grasper—

LINGLEY. Silence, sir! For goodness' sake, silence! I shan't be able to concentrate after this interruption. I came here for peace, damn you. I've been thinking too hard as it is—and now this little gnat—he's destroyed what I'd nearly completed in my mind. Damn you, sir, I'm sick of opposition. Damn you—you— (*The long low siren is heard again.*) Oh, my God! (*Falls into chair.*)

DUKE. Mr. Lingley, what is it? (*Goes to Lingley.*)

(TOM *goes to* LINGLEY *glass in hand.*)

LINGLEY. Wait—wait!

DUKE. You're looking ill.

LINGLEY. Yes, I am ill, I'm feeling ill, I am. Suddenly. I must have help, I was warned about this. An arm, please—and some of that stuff you're drinking.

(TOM *gives him drink and supports him.*)

Thank you. I shall be all right in a minute.

DUKE. I'll get the doctor.

LINGLEY. No. He'll only irritate me. I know what to do. I've been told what to do. Absolute quiet and fresh air. I'll go on deck. (*Feels in pocket.*) Oh yes, I'd forgotten. I'm to take one of these. (TOM *takes phial from his pocket and gives him a tabloid.*) Thank you. I must keep quiet, calm and not think. I shall be all right in a minute, and I'll see another man the moment I get to—get to— (*Looks from one to the other.*) Where *am* I going to?

DUKE. Marseilles you said, sir.

LINGLEY. Oh, yes, of course, Marseilles. (*Pause.*) What am I going to Marseilles for?

DUKE. Don't worry now.

LINGLEY. No, don't worry, that's right. I felt quite faint for the moment, Mr. Duke; your drink has done me good. I'll go on deck and sit down.

DUKE. I'll see you there.

LINGLEY. Thank you. I prefer to be alone. I'm quite all right. I shall soon remember everything. I know what I'm doing. Oh, I've forgotten my papers.

(DUKE *supports him towards the centre door.*)

DUKE. Leave them—they can wait—I'll look after them.

LINGLEY.   No, no, give them to me.

(TOM *gives them.*)

DUKE.   I wish you'd let me come and—

LINGLEY.   Please don't worry me! It's all right this time, I know it is, if I'm not worried. Thank you. I know what I'm doing, of course—I know—already I'm better. I'm going to meet someone, that's all. But was it Aaronson or was it Bantock?

DUKE.   Remember what your doctor said, don't worry!

LINGLEY.   (*Going towards the door.*) Of course not—no. That was the worst attack I've had so far. But I'm better now—yes—and the quiet and

[50]

sea air will soon clear my mind completely. Thank
you. I wish I could remember if it was Aaronson
or Bantock! Thank you, Mr. Duke, for your very
kind assistance.

(*He goes out slowly on to the deck and passes out of
sight to the right.* DUKE *follows up after him.*)

TOM. Padre!

DUKE. (*Stopping.*) Well?

TOM. What was it?

DUKE. I don't know—some sudden sort of
attack—I'm going to stop by him. (*Starting to follow* LINGLEY.)

TOM. Padre!

DUKE. Well? (*Returning.*)

TOM. It was my fault, I suppose.

DUKE. Oh no, I—

TOM. Are you angry with me?

DUKE. Why should I be?

TOM. You know.

DUKE. Drink is a terrible—

TOM. It seemed to do *him* good.

DUKE. That's different.

[51]

TOM.   You promised no sermons, anyway.

DUKE.   What made you start it?

TOM.   You said everyone should be keen on something.   Drink's my hobby.   Let's leave it at that.

DUKE.   Please don't joke about it.

TOM.   All right.   If you won't be angry with me—I hate people to be angry with me.   But I wasn't joking.

DUKE.   I'll see you later.   In fact I hope to see a lot of you on the voyage.   (*Starting out centre.*)

TOM.   Thanks.   That's what I said to the steward.   (*Stopping him again.*)   Padre!

DUKE.   (*Returning.*)   Well—well!

TOM.   One moment.

DUKE.   What is it?

TOM.   In strict confidence—now we're friends again—has it struck you by any chance that there's anything queer about this boat?   Strictly between ourselves.

DUKE.   No, it hasn't.

TOM. It has me.

DUKE. How do you mean?

TOM. I think there's something jolly queer about her. By Jove, if I were right it *would* be a joke!

DUKE. I don't follow you.

TOM. It's difficult to explain. But Mr. Lingley—and—and—oh, I'm not quite sure myself. It may be only my—

DUKE. Imagination?

TOM. Exactly. Only somehow I don't think it is.

DUKE. Go on. I must hurry.

TOM. Yes. Well (*turns to* DUKE), there was a sort of charwoman here just now—you didn't see her—a very decent sort of soul, of course, but—well—hardly the kind of person you'd expect to find here. And she couldn't remember where she was going. Excepting she was going to meet someone. (*Turns to him.*) Now this Lingley fellow's just told us the same thing in different words. He couldn't remember where he was going either, at least not clearly. And I've noticed lots of other little things. For instance, it's absurd sailing with our passenger list—there are so few of us. I tell you it's queer—and—

Duke.   Really I can't follow you.

Tom.   Then there's old Mrs. Banks drivelling on about joining her husband— Good Lor'! It's just struck me.

Duke.   What has?

Tom.   Colonel Cliveden-Banks kicked the bucket over a month ago. Surely she can't have forgotten *that*. Or—or would *that* be her father?

Duke.   Mr. Prior, if you take my advice, you'll follow Mr. Lingley's example and get some fresh air on deck.

Tom.   Yes, I think I will. All the same it *is* queer. (*Rises to above table.*) Certain you're not angry with me?

Duke.   Oh yes, certain. Shipmates, eh? (*Shakes hands.*)

Tom.   Oh yes, shipmates. But I bet you cut me the moment we land.

Duke.   Rot!

(*He follows* Lingley *on to the deck.* Henry *has entered and is lighting his pipe from a match which he has taken from the table up left.*)

Tom. Excuse me, sir, after you. (*Coming up to him, takes his match and lights his cigarette from it.*) Thanks. I say, do you mind if I ask you a question?

Henry. Of course not.

Tom. It's rather a queer question.

Henry. Go on.

Tom. Do—you—know—where—you—are—going—to?

Henry. Are you a Salvation Army man or what?

Tom. No, I'm quite serious.

Henry. Of course I know where I'm going to.

Tom. On this boat?

Henry. Certainly.

Tom. Thank goodness! I'm going to get some fresh air!

(*He goes out on to the deck.* Henry *goes up towards the deck, looks out.* Ann *enters left.*)

Ann. Why did you run away?

Henry. Wanted a match.

Ann. I had some.

[55]

HENRY. A bit nervy, too. (*Coming down centre.*)

ANN. You've no need to be now—we've sailed.

HENRY. Really!

ANN. Yes. I saw the water moving by the porthole.

HENRY. (*Runs up centre and looks out.*) You're right. Why, we're well out. Almost open water.

ANN. Yes, dear.

HENRY. Give me your hand.

ANN. Hold tight to it.

HENRY. Queer. It's just like an ordinary sailing.

ANN. Is it? (*Pause.*)

HENRY. A man just now asked me if I knew where I was going. I said I did.

ANN. That was right.

HENRY. Funny question though, wasn't it?

ANN. Oh, I don't know.

HENRY. He said it was queer. You don't think he—

ANN. Of course not, dear. Can you smell the sea? (*Crosses below settee.*)

HENRY. Yes, fine, isn't it?

ANN. I hope it will be terribly rough with lots of spray and wind.

HENRY. Why?

ANN. You can hold me closer.

HENRY. Ann! Ann! I've been worrying, I've been thinking just now—these modern inventions that doctors have—and things like that, you know.

ANN. You prosaic old thing—aren't you?

HENRY. They couldn't possibly call us back even now, could they?

ANN. Of course not, dear. How could they? We're safe enough as long as we hold tight.

HENRY. It was a risk, though, wasn't it?

ANN. Yes, dear.

HENRY. If—supposing—if it hadn't happened.

ANN. My dear, we always knew it would.

HENRY. Yes, but if it hadn't.

ANN. But we knew.

HENRY.   I think you were always more certain than I was.

ANN.   (*Sits.*)   Well then, I knew for both of us.

HENRY.   (*Sits.*)   Yes, that's right.   You knew. Ann, I trust you so in things I can't quite understand.   Of course I trust you in things I can understand, too.   But you seem to know so much more about the big things than I do.

ANN.   Perhaps I only pretend to.

HENRY.   Oh no, you know all right.   Give me another light, will you?   (*Bus.*)   Thanks.   It's nice being able to smoke.   Ann?

ANN.   Well, dear.

HENRY.   You're quite, quite sure?

ANN.   Quite sure, dear.

HENRY.   Isn't ours a terribly big secret?

ANN.   Isn't it?

HENRY.   Yes, Ann, I love you.

ANN.   I love you, Henry.

HENRY.   Always?

ANN.   Always.

HENRY.   Ann, I wonder how the dog is?

Ann. You baby—poor old Jock! Oh, they'll look after him all right.

Henry. I hope so. I say, Ann, when dogs die, what do you think happens to them?

Ann. I dunno. There must be a heaven for dogs—at least there ought to be.

Henry. What a jolly place it must be! No cats in it, of course.

Ann. Of course not. Just lots of bones and meat and water. And hot fires to lie in front of in the winter.

Henry. What about the kind masters?

Ann. I'd forgotten them. Oh, I expect there's some arrangement so that the good dogs can't remember the kind masters.

Henry. *We* remember, though.

Ann. Yes. *You* were a very kind master.

Henry. (*Rises.*) It's queer. (*Over to centre.*) Poor old Jock. (*Turns.*) I say, Ann, you don't think—

Ann. What?

Henry. Any of these other people can possibly know.

Ann. Our secret? Of course they can't.

HENRY. It *is* a wonderful secret.

ANN. (*Rises.*) I told you, Henry, how it would be as long as we believed.

HENRY. And yet? (*Over to her.*) I wonder if it's safe—even now.

ANN. What makes you say that?

HENRY. I can't quite remember, Ann, not clearly, not yet—it's coming back gradually of course, but—but—

ANN. Yes, dear?

HENRY. Ann, haven't you and I sinned in some way?

ANN. We've been true to each other. How can we have sinned?

HENRY. If we had, Ann, could they separate us?

ANN. Hold my hand tightly.

HENRY. I'm trying so hard to remember.

ANN. What, dear?

HENRY. What it is we've done that isn't right.

ANN. We've done nothing that isn't right.

HENRY. No. Not in our light, of course. But have we from other—from the world's—

ANN. We've never cared for the world. We're not going to care for it now.

HENRY. If we were wrong and if it were something very, very wrong, they couldn't separate us, could they?

ANN. That sort of thing's all over now, Henry. You've forgotten our secret.

HENRY. No, I haven't, it's all perfect, of course—excepting this one thing. (TOM *enters from the deck and unobserved by them stands quietly at the back leaning against doorway.*) Don't laugh—don't laugh at me, Ann, I'm only trying to remember, and asking for your help. But it seems (*sits*) to me this thing—this crime, if it is one—that we've committed, is something big, and yet that it's—now don't laugh—that it's only something to do with gas.

ANN. (*Sits beside him.*) Gas?

HENRY. Yes.

ANN. You silly.

HENRY. It seems to me that before we left the flat—

ANN. Our sad little flat!

HENRY. I forgot—to turn off—the gas.

ANN. You terrible silly! Of course you did. We—agreed—that. That's what we agreed.

[61]

HENRY. There's nothing very wrong in not turning off gas!

ANN. Don't worry, dear. Take my hand.

HENRY. Nothing so bad that they could separate us for it. You can't blame people for not turning off gas! And yet, I'd have sworn—Ann, you're quite certain that there isn't something else we've done? Something big?

ANN. There's nothing else, dear, I'm certain. You've nothing to be ashamed of.

HENRY. I love you so.

ANN. Thank you, Henry. Don't worry, dear.

HENRY. I wish I could remember *how* we got here. We wanted to so long. Anyway, now we have.

ANN. Let's go out on to the deck.

HENRY. Yes, let's—bless you. (*Both turn and see* TOM.) Hello, sir.

TOM. (*Quietly.*) Hello!

HENRY. We didn't notice you—

TOM. It's all right. I just came back to—

HENRY. May I introduce my wife? Ann, this is the gentleman who asked me if I knew where I was going.

Ann. How do you do?

Tom. How do you do?

(Tom *is a changed man. His tone is quiet and sad, and he stands perfectly rigid. The awful truth which has dawned upon him has completely sobered him. There is a pause. Then* Ann *goes out on to the deck, and* Henry *follows her.*)

Henry. (*As he exits.*) We'll see you later. We've sailed, you know.

(Scrubby *appears behind the bar.*)

Tom. Yes, I am right. (*Comes to bar.*) Scrubby!

Scrubby. Yes, sir?

Tom. I am right, aren't I, Scrubby?

Scrubby. Right, sir, in the head, do you mean?

Tom. You know what I mean.

Scrubby. Right about what, sir?

Tom. You—I—all of us on this boat.

Scrubby. What about all of us on this boat, sir?

Tom. (*Trembling with apprehension.*) We are—now answer me truthfully—we are all *dead, aren't we?*

[63]

SCRUBBY. (*After a pause. Very quietly with firm conviction.*) Yes, sir, we are all dead. Quite dead. They don't find out so soon as you have as a rule.

TOM. (*Pause.*) Queer! (*Sits left of table.*)

SCRUBBY. Not when you get used to it, sir.

TOM. How long have you been—you been—oh, you know?

SCRUBBY. Me, sir? Oh, I was lost young.

TOM. You were what?

SCRUBBY. Lost young, sir.

TOM. I don't understand.

SCRUBBY. No, sir, you wouldn't, not yet. But you'll get to know lots of things as the voyage goes on.

TOM. Tell me—tell me one thing—*now*.

SCRUBBY. Anything I can, sir.

TOM. (*Terrified.*) Where—where are we sailing for?

SCRUBBY. Heaven, sir. (*Pause.*) And hell, too. (*Pause.*) It's the same place, you see.

(*The curtain falls, with* TOM, *in a state of dreadful apprehension, gazing blankly at* SCRUBBY.)

ACT II

ACT II

The scene is unchanged, but it is evening. The curtains are drawn over the portholes, and the electric lights are on. The centre door is open from time to time, and it is pitch black outside.

On the left is seated MRS. CLIVEDEN-BANKS *in evening frock.* MR. LINGLEY *is with her, seated at the table on the right.*

LINGLEY. Well, I'm feeling very much better.

MRS. C-BANKS. I am so glad.

LINGLEY. I didn't quite catch your name at dinner. Being introduced during the soup has its disadvantages. The lady sitting next to us made it a little difficult to hear concisely.

MRS. C-BANKS. Mrs. Cliveden-Banks. Yes, I foresaw trouble with her this morning. Er— Mrs. Midget.

LINGLEY. Thank you. I say, Mrs. Midget.

MRS. C-BANKS. No, no! No. *I* am Cliveden-Banks.

LINGLEY. I apologise. What strikes me is that

this line can't be paying any dividends— Why, there's nobody on board.

Mrs. C-Banks.   Bother dividends as long as I'm comfortable!

Lingley.   This I think *is* the best place.

Mrs. C-Banks.   Quite a jolly little snuggery.

(The Reverend William Duke *enters and comes down centre.*)

At least it *was.*

Lingley.   Join me in a cigar, Duke?

Reverend W. Duke.   Thank you.

Mrs. C-Banks (*after a glance at* Duke.)   And I was so comfortable.   Where on earth can I go to now, I wonder?   (*Rises.*)

Lingley.   Oh! don't go.

Duke.   I hope you are not leaving on my account?

Mrs. C-Banks.   Your hope is shattered, young man, I am.

Duke.   Mrs. Cliveden-Banks, I don't know what I've done to offend you.   I can't help being a parson.   But I do know that you'll make it very uncomfortable for the others if you go on like this. So come, look over my shortcomings just for the trip. Remember that "to err is human, to forgive divine."

MRS. C-BANKS. Are you suggesting I have ever erred?

DUKE. In your case, I am certain such a thing would be impossible.

MRS. C-BANKS. Oh! very well. I sacrifice myself for the others' sake, I am a generous woman. How do you do? (*Shaking hands.*) But remember, Mr. Duke, if you *do* drown us all, I'll never speak to you again. (*Sits on settee.*)

DUKE. Splendid! (*Sits right of table right.*) Now, where are those other two? We might get up some bridge. We *must* all do something our first night out.

MRS. C-BANKS. What other two do you mean?

DUKE. They—er—at dinner. They sat by themselves. Seemed awfully nice—quiet. I don't know their names—I think the girl's called Ann.

MRS. C-BANKS. Oh! that couple! Oh! dear! Did you like the look of *them?*

DUKE. Yes, didn't you?

MRS. C-BANKS. No, I thought there was something funny about them.

LINGLEY. "Funny"?

Duke.   What do you mean by that?

Mrs. C-Banks.   I don't know.   It just struck me they were funny.   Not nice.   I may be wrong.   I hope I am.   But that *is* my opinion.   Not nice. Funny.

(Mrs. Midget *wanders in from the deck.   Now hatless.*)

Mrs. Midget.   May I come in?

Mrs. C-Banks.   Now I *shall* go.

Duke (*rises*).   Yes, come in, Mrs. Midget, come in.

Mrs. Midget (*entering*).   It's a bit lonely in the street.

Duke.   "Street"?

Mrs. Midget.   Out there.

Mrs. C-Banks.   She means the deck—how quaint.

Duke.   It's more cheerful in here, isn't it?

Mrs. Midget.   Oh, much.

Duke.   Sit down.   You're not nervous, now, are you?

Mrs. Midget (*sits at table, right centre*).   Not of you, sir.   You wear just the same sort of collar

[70]

as our parson does. I wish I was back in the Lambeth Road.

MRS. C-BANKS (*to* LINGLEY). I can't stand the creature. I really can't—she's too impossible. I shall squash her. Good evening, Mrs. Midget. We heard you at dinner. Very warm, this evening, isn't it?

MRS. MIDGET. Yes, dearie. 'Ellish 'ot. Beggin' your Reverence's pardon. I've come out all of a sweat. (*Wiping her neck with handkerchief.*)

MRS. C-BANKS. Dear me! Have you really? How embarrassing. What a day you have had, haven't you? First of all you're struck into a heap and now you've come out all of a—yes, exactly. Yet, I suppose you travel a great deal?

MRS. MIDGET. Every day. Lambeth to the Bank and from the Bank back to Lambeth. Workin' in the City as I did—do.

MRS. C-BANKS. The City! How enthralling! Big financial interests, I presume?

MRS. MIDGET. No—charrin'. And in the old times we always managed Margate in the summer. Nice spot, Margate, ain't it?

MRS. C-BANKS. I know nothing against it. I have never been there, of course.

[71]

MRS. MIDGET.   Never been to Margate! (*To* DUKE.)   Would you believe it?

DUKE.   Yes.

MRS. MIDGET.   Oh! you'd love Margate a treat, mum.   What with the paddling and everything.   Do you like cocoanuts?

MRS. C-BANKS.   Cocoanuts?   Oh, good Lord no!

MRS. MIDGET.   Ah!   Then you mightn't like Margate.   They grow very good ones there though. At least they used to.   Cors' I ain't been there since I lost all my money.   Do you know, all of yer, believe me or believe me not, I once had a house of my very own.

MRS. C-BANKS.   How magnificent!

MRS. MIDGET.   Yes, wasn't it?   Though of course it wasn't *all* my own.   No.   Semi-detached, and lodgers yer know.   Payin' guests and very well it *did* pay for donkey's years.   Well enough for me to make my son a gentleman anyway, and send him to college to prove it.

MRS. C-BANKS.   Quite romantic.   Perhaps I have met your dear boy?   Where is he now?   Cambridge or Cologne?

MRS. MIDGET.   Well, 'avin' become a gentleman 'e naturally lost all 'is money.   And 'is money was my money.   And I ain't seen him since.   'E hasn't

[72]

seen me, not to know me, since 'e was a little boy. I got my brother-in-law, 'e's rich, to take him over and manage things for me. You see I didn't want to disgrace 'im. 'E's been a good boy.

LINGLEY. Sounds it.

MRS. MIDGET (*resentfully*). 'E *was,* I tell yer. But you know what it is yerself, sir.

LINGLEY. I do not—I have never lost a penny in my life.

MRS. MIDGET. Ah! then you can't be a gentleman.

LINGLEY. What?

MRS. MIDGET. Now the gentlemen my—my boy mixed with *were* gents. Always broke, bless 'em, and then 'avin' "another one" just to make 'em forget about it. And my boy the life and soul of the 'ole crowd. At least so the letter told me from the brother-in-law. And you can't 'ave your cake and eat it, as the sayin' goes, nor your gin and drink it *as* you well know, sir.

LINGLEY. Confound it, madam, I do *not* know.

DUKE. Sorrow's sent to try us, Mrs. Midget.

MRS. MIDGET. Cors' it's sent to try us. What else could it be sent for? And it does try us very much.

[73]

DUKE.   Yes—but sometimes as in your case—

MRS. C-BANKS.   Mr. Duke means you would never have the steady poise, you would not be the woman of the world you so obviously are unless—

MRS. MIDGET.   You're trying to pull my leg, aren't you?

DUKE.   I'm afraid Mrs. Cliveden-Banks *was* trying to.   I certainly didn't mean that.

MRS. MIDGET.   Thank you, sir. (*Rises and crosses centre to* MRS. CLIVEDEN-BANKS.)   Mum, I may not know the manners of Society, and if them is such as yours I do *not* want to.   With which terse remark I shuts up, being sorry for anything I've said. (*Moves up centre.*)

DUKE.   Yes, yes, quite, quite.   Well, we must all *do* something, you know, time is getting on. What about those cards?

MRS. MIDGET (*coming down right*).   Oh! I'd love a game o' cards. (*Sits.*)   Mr. Prior was only telling me this afternoon before 'e—well, 'e was telling me that 'e played cards.

LINGLEY.   Prior—pooh!

MRS. MIDGET.   I like 'im anyway.

DUKE.   Very unfortunate—Prior— Yes, yes, dear, dear, dear.

MRS. C-BANKS. Poor Mr. Prior! But I hear he's always like that nowadays. A thoroughly bad lot in fact. Not that I would say so in public of course—but just between ourselves I mean. Oh! (*Laughs.*) What a sight he was and what an exhibition he made of himself. I shall never forget it. Never! (*Laughs again.*) Mr. Lingley, he called you a—dear, dear me—I can't help smiling but he called you a— (*laughs*) didn't he?

LINGLEY. Never mind what he called me, madam.

MRS. C-BANKS. Well, you *are* rather like one, you know, if you don't mind my saying so. Where is he now, I wonder?

LINGLEY. Sleeping it off if he's a wise man.

DUKE. Which he isn't.

MRS. C-BANKS. He wasn't at dinner naturally. I expect you all noticed it.

DUKE. Of course, of course. It's a great shame, a great pity. (TOM *enters; he is very pale, tense and very quiet.*) Ah! Prior!

MRS. C-BANKS. Mr. Prior! Why, we were just talking about you—

TOM. Indeed.

MRS. C-BANKS. Yes, I was only saying what a steady hand—

[75]

Tom. Don't waste any more of your breath than is absolutely necessary, Mrs. Cliveden-Banks. Nor any of you, either.

Mrs. C-Banks. I beg your pardon.

Duke. What's the matter now?

Tom. We're trapped, that's all.

Duke (*rises*). Trapped!

Tom. Yes, trapped. Every one of us—all of us on this boat, we're done for.

Mrs. C-Banks. What, *already!* (*Threateningly pointing to* Duke.) Mr. *Duke! !*—

Tom. I mean it. You needn't believe me if you don't want to. It's true all the same. We're dead people!

Lingley. Oh, run away, run away, young man, and sleep it off.

Tom. I'm sober enough now. And the boat's not sinking. I don't mean that either.

Lingley. What in blazes do you mean then, sir?

Tom. Duke, come here. Feel my pulse. Draw a chalk line on the floor and make me walk it if you want to. (Duke *moves up to him.*) Look at my eyes. Now—I am sober, aren't I?

DUKE. Yes, I think so.

TOM. The last time I heard a clergyman say "Yes, I think so" was on the music halls. Funny I shall never go to a music hall again.

MRS. MIDGET (*rises*). Why doesn't someone put the poor young man to bed? It would be much kinder.

TOM. Quiet, please. I don't want to frighten you—any of you—but I feel—I ought to try and convince you. You admit I'm sober. You'll have to take my word I'm not mad.

LINGLEY. I should want more than your word for that.

TOM. You shall have it. You shall have the word of the—the man who calls himself a steward, and the words of two of our fellow passengers. The two who I see are not here.

LINGLEY. But what about, sir? What are you driving at?

TOM (*comes down left centre*). I began to suspect this morning before lunch. Nobody seemed to know where they were going to. I'd forgotten myself, though I didn't admit it. I didn't want to. I didn't dare to. I daren't now. When I was quite convinced, I got drunk. That was only natural. All my life I've started to face facts by getting drunk. Well—when—when I woke up again—about an hour ago, you were all in the saloon. I was frightened, terribly frightened. At last I got out of my cabin and went over the ship. I made myself. Yes, over her, all over her. Into the officers' quarters and everything. No one said a word to me for a very simple reason. There's no one on board *to* say anything. No captain, no crew, no nothing.

Mrs. C-Banks. If there's *no* crew on board this ship, Mr. Prior, may I ask who waited on *me* at dinner?

Tom. There's no one at all on board this ship, excepting we five—and those two—and the steward. *He* waited on you at dinner. He's in charge of the ship. I made myself find out. Do you know where that steward is now? He's in the rigging—sitting cross-legged—high up in the rigging. I've just seen him.

Mrs. Midget. It's takin' 'im in a funny way, ain't it?

Duke (*advancing on* Tom). Really, Prior, I think that—

Tom (*turning to* Duke). I don't know what I'm talking about? Very well, then, answer me this. Who have you, any of you, seen on board this ship since she sailed? Excepting ourselves? Mrs. Midget, perhaps you can help. (*Going to* Mrs. Midget.) When I sent you to your stewardess this morning, did you see her?

Mrs. Midget. See who? I saw no one except the fellow I went with. And first rate he looked after me. Got me a cup of tea and—

Tom. I tell you I— (*Turns to* Duke.) Padre— Padre, think carefully, who exactly have *you* spoken to?

Duke. I—really, I—I have seen men about of course.

Tom. Have you? Have you indeed? What sort of men, sailors?

Duke. Yes, I think so.

Tom. In the same way that you thought I was sober.

Mrs. C-Banks. You don't expect us to talk to sailors, do you, Mr. Prior, able bodied though they may be?

Tom. Have any of you met anybody else then? A purser, an officer of any sort, even a stoker?

Lingley. That reminds me. In your gigantic tour of this vessel did you by any chance strike the engine room?

TOM. No, I couldn't find it.

LINGLEY. A pity! I'd hoped you were going to say the ship was worked by elastic—ha, ha, ha.

(MRS. CLIVEDEN-BANKS *laughs also*.)

TOM. Joke if you want to. If that *is* a joke. Well, Padre, speak up.

DUKE. Well, I—I must have met someone of course.

TOM. You *should* have met someone, you mean. But you've not. Padre, where are *you* landing?

DUKE. Landing? I'm going to—of course I'm going to—mind your own business.

TOM. *Where are you landing?*

DUKE. I'm taking a little holiday, that's all. I'm going first to—to—

TOM. You see you can't remember. I'm right! I knew I was. Why, look at the quiet way we sailed. Was anybody here to see any of us off? No, you know they weren't. Because you can't see people off—not right off—to where we're going.

LINGLEY. I wish you'd get out, sir; we want to play cards.

TOM. Cards—pah! Lingley, Lingley (*down to* LINGLEY), you're impossible! Why I should try

[80]

to warn *you*, I don't know.   Still, can you really, honestly, tell me you've seen nothing queer about this boat?

Lingley.   Nothing whatever—excepting you. She's exactly the same as any other boat—go away.

Tom.   Is she?   Is she indeed?

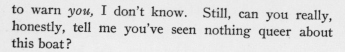

(Henry *and* Ann *appear at the centre door and cross down left.   They are, as ever, close together and almost always hand in hand, and aloof from the others.*)

Tom.   Well, I'll tell you one little thing I noticed about her that struck me as slightly different.   This boat doesn't carry a port light—no—and she doesn't carry a starboard one either!   *Now* is she the same as any other?   *Now* can you settle down to your cards?

Lingley.   You *are* mad?

Tom.   Go and look then!   Get on deck.   You can find out if you go forward for yourself, and if you can see 'em—you're mad.

Lingley.   I shouldn't make such a fool of myself.

Tom (*seeing* Ann *and* Henry).   Ah!—you're just in time.

Henry.   What for?

TOM.   To give these people their chance—to stop them from making fools of themselves—to back me up.

HENRY.   I don't quite follow.

TOM.   You know—you knew this morning.

HENRY.   Knew what?

TOM.   You've been on deck?

HENRY.   Just now.

TOM.   Notice anything wrong?   (*A pause.*)

HENRY.   With what?

TOM.   Oh! don't pretend—don't lie to me.

HENRY.   Really, I *don't* understand.

TOM.   Then you don't understand how you got here, either, I suppose?   How either of you got here. (*Up to them.*)   Gas, my dear sir, sheer gas.

ANN.   Henry, don't speak to him!   (*Moves down a step.*)   He frightens me.

TOM.   Yes, I suppose I do.   I know as well, you see.

MRS. C-BANKS.   He's trying to frighten us, that's all.

LINGLEY.   Madam, I must apologise for our fellow passenger.   He—he is not—ahem—well.

TOM (*moves down a step*). Of course I'm not well. Under the circumstances I should have thought that would have been obvious.

LINGLEY (*rises*). Mr. Duke, I see an unpleasant duty will have to be performed. As a clergyman you must be more used to unpleasantness than any of us. Will you please perform it.

DUKE. What do you want me to do?

LINGLEY. Get him to the doctor—or lock him up.

(DUKE *moves slightly to centre door.*)

TOM (*up to centre door*). The doctor! I tell you there *is* no doctor. No one! And if you try any of that sort of thing on, I'll make trouble.

MRS. C-BANKS. Oh, dear, how selfish.

TOM. But I tell you what you *can* do if you like—

LINGLEY. Well?

TOM. I'll make a bargain with you.

LINGLEY. What is it?

TOM. Go out there—one of you men and convince yourselves about those lights. Then if I'm wrong—well, I'll go quietly.

MRS. MIDGET. That seems fair, poor fellow.

Tom. Well? What do you say? Mr. Lingley, will you oblige?

Lingley. I should never dream of interfering with the ship's discipline.

Tom (*to* Henry). It's no good asking *you,* of course?

Henry. No.

Tom. Padre—you're the only one left—what do you say?

Duke. If I do it—just to satisfy you—you'll keep your word?

Tom. Yes.

Duke. Very well then.

Lingley. Preposterous! (*Sits on settee.*)

Tom. Thank you. (Duke *goes slowly to doorway.*) Oh! Duke, the truth.

Duke. Of course.
    (Duke *goes quietly out on to the deck.*)

Lingley. Weak, weak.

Mrs. C-Banks. Ah! the Church was always like that!

Tom. Don't you run the Church down so. Take

my advice, you may want her help very badly before long. Wait until I'm proved right.

MRS. C-BANKS. I simply ignore you, Mr. Prior. You won't be right. That is why I ignore you.

(DRAKE'S *drum is faintly heard, a heavily muffled and mysterious and irregular beating.*)

LINGLEY. Childish weak foolishness giving in to you. *I've* never given in to anyone. No one's ever given in to me. I should never expect them to. You're drunk, sir, and you're in the wrong, sir, and—

(*The drum stops.*)

TOM. Quiet. (*Rises.*) I can hear something —out there.

HENRY. What is it?

TOM. Wait a minute—it's stopped now.

LINGLEY. I didn't hear anything.

TOM. I did. It sounded like a drum.

LINGLEY. A drum?

TOM. Yes. A muffled drum.

MRS. C-BANKS. Very possibly it *was* a muffled drum.

LINGLEY. Very possibly it was imagination.

MRS. C-BANKS. What's the good of talking about things out there in the cold, anyway? Let's concentrate on making it nice and comfortable in here for our cards, (*to* TOM) which we hope to start the moment you've gone.

TOM (*moving towards her*). Mrs. Cliveden-Banks, you're an ostrich! I'm sorry, but you are. You're in danger, great danger of something out there—something, I don't know what it is—but it may affect your very soul—yet all you can think about is light and warmth and cards in here. So the only word for you *is* ostrich.

LINGLEY (*to* MRS. C-BANKS). Dear me, dear me, I can't help smiling, but he called you a—didn't he?

ANN (*looking out on to the deck*). Oh! why doesn't he come back? (*In terrified impatience.*)

HENRY. Steady, steady. (*To others.*) My wife is easily upset. (*Draws her away from door.*)

MRS. MIDGET. Poor dear.

LINGLEY. It's too bad of you, Prior.

TOM. Is it?

ANN. What has happened to him?

TOM. To whom?

ANN. The clergyman—of course.

[86]

TOM. Oh! Duke! Who knows? Perhaps he can't get back. He's only been a second away.

ANN. You don't think— (*Drum starts again, beating irregularly and a trifle more loudly.*)

TOM. I don't think, because I don't know any more than you do. Hark! (*A pause.*) Listen, there it is again. The drum!

LINGLEY. Um! *I* must be getting deaf!

(DUKE *appears as if breathless—a pause. He is pale and agitated, terrified—but tries to conceal it.*)

TOM (*tensely anxious*). Well—well?

LINGLEY. Well—speak, Mr. Duke. (*A pause.*)

ANN (*with a great effort at dissembling*). It's— all right, of course.

LINGLEY. Duke? (*Another pause.*) It *is* all right?

DUKE. Of course.

LINGLEY. Everything?

DUKE. Everything.

(*Drum stops.*)

MRS. C-BANKS. I knew it would be all the time.

[87]

Tom (*rushing up and throwing himself on* Duke). You liar! You liar! Come with me—I'll show you. (*Grabs him by throat.*)

(Lingley *rises.*)

Duke (*struggling with him*). Prior! (Mrs. Midget *rises.* Lingley *seizes* Tom's *neck.* Ann *and* Henry *up left huddled together in alarm.*) You promised to go quietly.

Tom. You swore to tell the truth! *You clergyman,* you dirty liar!

Duke. Got him, Lingley?

Tom (*struggling violently*). I'll show you! No more lies! Now we're dead, you bloody liar! I won't be cheated! I *will* make you understand! I'm trying to help, I tell you—I'm only trying to help—

Lingley. Be quiet, sir.

(*They bring* Tom *to chair left of table right. He sinks to chair and with head buried in arms on table sobs hysterically but quietly—exhausted.*)

Mrs. C-Banks. Well, if I'm wanted, I'll be in the ladies' waiting room. (*Going left.*) A long letter, you know, while the details are still fresh. (*Turns.*) Coming, dear? (*Sees she is speaking to* Mrs. Midget—*turns at door.*) Oh, no! (*She goes out with her nose in the air.* Mrs. Midget *crosses and exits left following* Mrs. Cliveden-Banks.

(*All stand quietly for a moment's pause.*)

Henry (*to* Ann). Dear?

Ann (*as she goes*). I'll wait on deck. (*Exit centre.*)

Lingley (*to* Henry). Shut those doors.

(Henry *closes centre door.*)

Lingley. And now, sir.

Duke (*coming down to* Prior). Prior, I apologise.

Lingley. What do you mean?

Duke. That Mr. Prior was perfectly right.

Lingley. What?

Duke. There *is* no—there's no starboard—no—

Lingley. There's *not!*

Duke. No. There's no light on the boat at all. She's black as pitch.

Lingley. Impossible.

Duke. Look for yourself.

Lingley (*alarmed now, crosses to centre door, opens it and glances out into the dark, then shuts it. Then hesitates and turns*). But—the bridge?

Duke. As far as I could see there's nothing—nothing anywhere.

Lingley. Nothing—nobody?

Duke. I'm not even certain that we're moving.

Lingley (*coming back.*) Good heavens, man, why didn't you tell us this at once?

Duke. I didn't want to alarm the ladies.

Lingley. Women drown as easily as men.

Duke. Is this a question of drowning? Something must be done—we must all *do* something immediately.

Tom. Exactly, but what?

Lingley (*thoroughly rattled*). To begin with—well—somebody—somebody ought to ring a bell.

Tom. And get someone else to explain.

Lingley. Duke—do you—do you believe in all this?

Duke. I don't understand it.

Lingley (*to* Henry). And you, sir?

Henry. I don't understand it either.

Tom. That's not true! And you know it's not true!

[90]

DUKE. Prior! Now look here, when did you first feel certain, in your mind, about all this?

TOM (*pointing at* HENRY—*sits at table*). After I'd heard something he said. I spoke to the steward, I asked him if—he told me the truth, I'm sure—it seems we're sailing for (*pause*)—both Hell and Heaven.

DUKE. Very interesting from a professional point of view, of course.

TOM. If there's anything else you want to know, better ask *him, the steward.* (*Goes toward bar.*)

DUKE. Where is he now, I wonder?

LINGLEY. Still sitting high up in the rigging, I expect.

TOM. Don't be sarcastic! He was there.

LINGLEY. Was he? (*Rises, takes one step towards* TOM.) Then how did you see him if it's all dark outside?

TOM (*vaguely*). That never struck me. But he was there.

(SCRUBBY *enters from left and softly strolls across towards centre.*)

DUKE (*rises*). We must hurry. Whilst we're talking like this we may be drifting on to the rocks —crashing into something or—

SCRUBBY (*always very kindly, very quiet and compassionate—like a tolerant elder to children.*) No, sir, you won't do that.

LINGLEY. Now look here, my man. What is all this nonsense? I can't stand excitement. My doctor ordered rest and quiet. Where's the captain? Take me to him.

SCRUBBY. Oh, he left long ago, sir.

LINGLEY. Enough of that! Understand? By Gad, when I get back to London I'll report—

SCRUBBY. I'm afraid you won't get back to London, sir—

LINGLEY. No more of your impertinence! Take me to the captain!—do you hear? You're only a damned servant—take me to him—

DUKE. Mr. Lingley, I think we should *all* keep our tempers.

SCRUBBY. That's all right, sir, I've known a lot of them to get angry at first. (*Crossing to right.*)

LINGLEY. A lot of whom?

SCRUBBY. People like you, sir, who are just beginning.

LINGLEY. Beginning?

SCRUBBY. To be passengers.

Tom. What you told me this morning *was* true, wasn't it?

Scrubby. That we're dead, sir? Yes, quite dead if that's what you mean.

Lingley. You speak for yourself.

Duke. It *is* queer. (*Sits right of table right.*)

Scrubby. Why, sir? We didn't think it was queer when we were born.

Lingley. Now listen. I don't want any mysteries.

Scrubby. There are none, sir.

Lingley. And I mean to get in touch with someone at once—ah! I have it, the wireless!

Scrubby. She doesn't carry any, sir.

Lingley. That's illegal anyway! Duke! (*A pause.*) Duke?

Duke. I'm afraid I can't suggest anything.

Lingley. But—but—! (*Suddenly overcome with fear.*) I must get out of this—I must get out of it.

Scrubby. That, sir, is impossible until after the examination. (*Going behind bar.*)

Lingley. What examination?

[93]

SCRUBBY. You'll find out later, sir.

LINGLEY. The ladies ought to be warned immediately.

SCRUBBY. I should leave them to find out for themselves, sir, if I were you. I have known some of them not to like the idea to begin with and get hysterical. It is kinder to let them find out for themselves.

DUKE. They will find out?

SCRUBBY. Undoubtedly, sir.

LINGLEY (*suddenly seeing* HENRY). Damn it—don't stand there saying nothing—get upset!

HENRY. I am—of course.

LINGLEY. You're a bright lot, all of you, aren't you? So helpful—but—but—what are we to do? What are we to do? (*To* DUKE.) *You're* always talking about doing things? What are we to do?

DUKE. I really—don't know. Of course, if we were all quite certain—a prayer—

LINGLEY. Is praying going to bring the captain or the crew to life?

TOM. Or *any* of us for that matter.

SCRUBBY. There's no danger, gentlemen, if *that's* what you're frightened of.

LINGLEY. Isn't there?

SCRUBBY. No, sir.

LINGLEY. *I'm* not frightened.

DUKE. I am. How many times have *you* made this passage, steward?

SCRUBBY. About five thousand times, sir.

LINGLEY. Five—

SCRUBBY. Yes. I was lost young.

DUKE. And it's always been like this?

SCRUBBY. Not always, sir. No. As I was telling this gentleman (*referring to* PRIOR), the passengers don't find out so quickly as a rule. I suppose it's because of the half-ways we've got on board this trip.

DUKE. Half-ways?

SCRUBBY. Yes, sir, it sometimes *does* work like that.

LINGLEY. There is no point in standing here talking to a lunatic. The question is, "What is—?"

SCRUBBY. —to be done? That's what they *all* ask, sir. There's *nothing* to be done. Just go on as if nothing had happened.

TOM. How simple.

[95]

SCRUBBY. Quite, sir, quite. You'll find everything simple now. Until it comes to the examination.

LINGLEY. Don't talk to me as if I were a schoolboy.

SCRUBBY. It *is* rather like going to school, sir.

LINGLEY. Stop! It's all right. Everything's all right. I've solved the whole thing suddenly.

HENRY. Have you? (*Still up left aloof.*)

LINGLEY. Of course I have. I'm asleep. I'm safe really. I'm simply asleep.

TOM. What am I?—part of the nightmare?

LINGLEY. I've had dreams like this before. Go away, go away, all you people. It's no good your waiting! I'm Lingley of Lingley, Ltd. Not one of you can touch me. I turned myself into a company years ago. Only go away now. (*A pause and then he turns to the steward.*) *I am asleep,* aren't I?

SCRUBBY. Yes, sir—sound asleep—or just waking.

LINGLEY. Good, good. Now get away, get away, all you people. I shall go. (*Moves about settee.*) I will go. (*Crosses to door left.*) Isn't that lucky! I *can* go. You know, in *some* dreams, you can't.

(LINGLEY *walks off left.*)

[96]

SCRUBBY (*following him*). Don't worry, gentlemen, I'll look after him.

(SCRUBBY *follows him.*)

DUKE. A good sleep would be the very best thing for Lingley.

TOM. Would it?

DUKE. Eh?

TOM. Well, I mean—you know—would it help now?

DUKE. Oh! yes, of course—I'd forgotten—I really don't know. I—I don't understand. I'm quite a young man and there's such a lot of work to be done after my holiday.

TOM. Try some of this whiskey—it still seems to work. (*Going to bar.*)

DUKE (*rises*). No, I don't think I will if you'll excuse me, in case we—we meet anyone.

TOM (*toying idly with glass*). I'm awfully sorry. I'm afraid I'm a fearful rotter, I'm so used to it. Any crises you know— (*He sits on front of table.*) I say—I say— (*Pause.*) Charles Reade—or some other rotten novelist once said, "Never too late to mend," didn't he? Do you think there's any truth in novels? And then there was that other chap—the Great One, you know, in the Bible, he said—he—

There you are, you see; that's the sort of fellow I am! I've forgotten what *he* said.

DUKE. Does it really much matter what either of them said? Isn't it more to the point what *you* have got to say?

TOM. No sermons! But, if you please, I would like to talk to you seriously if you'd listen to me, out there in the dark.

DUKE (*rises*). Shall we go out there—in the dark—and talk to each other, shipmate?

TOM (*humorously*). This is a great chance for *you*, isn't it?

DUKE. We must both, my dear Prior, keep our sense of humour. (*Moves up to door centre. To* HENRY *at door*.) Coming out, sir? (*With* TOM *to door arm in arm*.)

HENRY. No, not yet. (*Still up left*.)

DUKE. See you later then. (*He goes out*.)

HENRY. Yes.

TOM. I say, your wife's out there, isn't she?

HENRY. Yes.

TOM. Shall I send her to you?

HENRY. Oh—thank you.

Tom (*returning a step from door*).   You must have known or you wouldn't have let her be out there alone.

Henry.   I knew *nothing*.   I know nothing now. Good night.

Tom.   I suppose so.   (*He walks out on to the deck and disappears.   There is a pause and then* Henry *calls "Ann!"   Another pause.   He calls again.*   Ann *enters from the deck.*)

Henry. Ann— (*A pause.*) Come here. (*Crosses right to above table.*)

Ann.   What is it?   (*She goes to left of* Henry.)

Henry.   Come here.

Ann.   I'm with you.

Henry.   Ann—listen—they know we're dead— they're—they're finding out our secret.

Ann (*frightened*).   I know!   I know they are! (*They look at each other.*)

Henry.   What will they *do* to us, dear?

Ann (*getting closer to him*).   They won't separate us—will they?

CURTAIN

ACT III

ACT III

SCENE I

It is an afternoon some days later. There is a small table near the bar with a water carafe and a glass, a hand bell and papers on it. Chairs are arranged round it in a circle as if for a meeting. Otherwise the scene is unchanged.

MR. LINGLEY is pacing up and down the room in an agitated manner, watch in hand.

LINGLEY. Four thirty—four thirty-*one!* Tut, tut, tut! (*Goes to table.*) Late, late. Now let's see— (*Counting the chairs.*) Mrs. Cliveden-Banks— Mr. Duke—two—four—six— (*Touching armchair at head and fingering water bottle.*) Myself here— yes, that's right. (*The siren is heard. Takes out watch again.*) Four thirty-one and a half—four thirty-*two.* Oh, tut, tut, tut! (*TOM walks in from the deck. LINGLEY stops in his walk on seeing him.*) Good gracious, fancy *you* being the first!

TOM. First for what?

LINGLEY. The meeting, sir!

TOM. Oh, I'd forgotten about your rotten old meeting.

LINGLEY.   Where are the others?

TOM.   On deck.   It may interest you to know we've just sighted land.   (*Sits at table.*)

LINGLEY.   Land, Mr. Prior?   Land!   (*Delighted.*)

TOM.   Yes.   We've just sighted *hell.*

LINGLEY.   Oh.

TOM.   It looks quite a jolly little spot from here. The padre's arranging a sweepstake on the exact time it will take us to get in.   He's suddenly developed a sense of humour.

LINGLEY.   Sense of humour and sweepstakes when we're all—all—!   What's the use of a sense of humour to a dead man?   (*Pacing to and fro, up and down.*)

TOM.   I dunno!   I've never asked one.

LINGLEY.   Oh, why don't they *come?*

TOM.   You're getting the wind up a bit, aren't you?   Oh, I don't blame you, Lingley of Lingley Limited, for I shouldn't be surprised if over there a nice private little gridiron isn't being warmed up for your personal reception.

LINGLEY.   Will you be quiet, you foolish boy!

(SCRUBBY *enters left.*)

[104]

SCRUBBY (*indicating the table*).   Everything correct, sir?

LINGLEY.   Eh?

SCRUBBY.   Enough chairs, sir?

LINGLEY.   Oh! yes, very nice indeed, very nice, Mr. Scrubby.   Er——here is half-a-crown for your trouble.   Thank you.

SCRUBBY.   Thank *you,* sir.

LINGLEY.   What for?   Half-a-crown is no use to me now.   Wait!   Please tell the others—the others—my shipmates—that they're late for the meeting.

SCRUBBY (*as he goes out centre.*)   Certainly, sir.

LINGLEY.   Thank you, Mr. Scrubby, thank you.

TOM.   What's the object of this meeting, anyway?

LINGLEY.   Can't you see?

TOM.   Yes.   That's why I asked.   (*To bar.*)

LINGLEY.   We're approaching our destination, and I want to make this one last effort.   I feel we should talk the matter over in a rational spirit—and as a business man I've called this meeting.

TOM.   You *would.*   And, as has probably been your custom, you think that a committee report and minutes, and balance sheets and all that bunkum may impress the examiner as they do shareholders and *other* examiners. Of course you'll be chairman?

LINGLEY. Naturally. I seem to be the only one qualified.

TOM. You admit it.

LINGLEY. By right of experience and proved ability—Prior, when I was a boy—

TOM. Were you ever a boy? Poor parents!

LINGLEY. When I was seventeen I could only manage one egg for breakfast.

TOM. I can never manage *any* breakfast myself.

LINGLEY. *Afford* one egg, I mean. At six thirty A.M. I used to walk to my work.

TOM. On the egg? (*Sits right.*)

LINGLEY. And after business I'd walk home again. That was the begininng of Lingley, Limited. When I was seventeen I made my motto "Try to rely on yourself." At thirty-seven I made it "Rely on yourself."

TOM. So you fired *me*.

LINGLEY. At forty-seven I made it "Rely on yourself *absolutely*"; because if you fail all your friends will only say, "It serves you right."

TOM. *Had* you any friends at forty-seven?

LINGLEY. You're incorrigible! And I thought *you* were concerned in this—this dilemma.

TOM. I *am*.

(MRS. CLIVEDEN-BANKS *enters through the centre door. She is in the very deepest mourning.*)

MRS. C-BANKS. I must apologise for being late! I've been playing sweepstake.

LINGLEY. Mrs. Cliveden-Banks! Why this dress?

MRS. C-BANKS. Our present circumstances!

(TOM *sits left. His attitude toward the subsequent proceedings is one of contempt.*)

LINGLEY. Will you sit here?

MRS. C-BANKS. It's nice to be able to, isn't it? (*Sits in the first chair left of table.*) And the object of this meeting, Mr. Lingley, is—er—?

LINGLEY. Well—er—is this company alive or dead?

TOM. And the next question on the agenda?

LINGLEY (*a pause; sits*). What is going to happen to us? Mr. Prior—as a prospective shareholder—I ask you what you think?

Tom. Lingley—do you know anything about Elizabethan furniture?

Lingley. Nothing whatever.

Tom. Neither do I. That's why I never talk about it.

Lingley. But it is the right thing to do, isn't it?

Tom. To solemnly sit down and discuss if we've immortal souls or if we haven't? And if we have, to pool 'em. (*Sarcastically.*) Undoubtedly. (*Rises.*) "We must combine"—the most hopeful refuge for an embarrassed business man like you.

Lingley. Exactly. We must all face this examiner together.

(Rev. W. Duke *enters. He is quite different and most cheerful.*)

Duke. Hello, Tom! Hello, Lingley! (*To* Mrs. Cliveden-Banks.) Hello, Banky!

Mrs. C-Banks. Banky!

Duke. Yes. (*He shakes her shoulders.*) Banky, Banky! We're dead now, so my job's over and I can be quite natural; do what I like and say what I like, Banky. (*Over* Lingley's *right shoulder.*) Prior, have you heard this one—I've been dying to spring it for ages—"There was a young girl of Hong-Kong."

[108]

MRS. C-BANKS (*convulsed with laughter*). Oh, *I* know that one.

LINGLEY. Sir! You ought to be ashamed of yourself. We are about to hold a Board Meeting.

DUKE. Sorry. I overheard one of my ex-choir boys reciting that in the Vestry. I remember his voice was breaking at the time. Damn badly. (*Sits below* TOM.)

LINGLEY. Supposing your Bishop heard you say "damn."

DUKE. Impossible, unless he's listening in.

LINGLEY. You've evidently become unbalanced.

MRS. MIDGET (*entering centre*). Is this the meeting 'ouse?

LINGLEY. Yes, Mrs. Midget. Sit here, will you? Very good of you to come. I hope you—your family are well and—

MRS. MIDGET (*sits at left of table below* MRS. CLIVEDEN-BANKS). What the 'ell are you talking about?

MRS. C-BANKS. Please do not mention hell, Mrs. Midget; it's rather a ticklish subject at the moment.

LINGLEY. Now, are we all here?

TOM. We're all here.

Mrs. Midget.   The young couple aren't 'ere.

Lingley.   *They* never say anything, anyway. Shall we begin?

Mrs. C-Banks.   Begin.

Lingley.   Very well, then.   (*Rises.*)   Ahem! (*Rings bell on table.*)

Tom.   They're off!

Lingley.   Ladies and gentlemen——

Mrs. Midget.   'Ear, 'ear!

Mrs. C-Banks.   Be quiet!

Mrs. Midget.   I was only thanking 'im for the compliment.

Lingley.   Ladies *and* gentlemen——"de mortuis nil nisi bonum."

Tom.   Oh, get on with it!

Lingley.   I intend to.   *Ladies* and gentlemen——I am a business man.

Duke.   Quite.

Lingley.   I have never done anything in my life without a reason.

Duke.   Quite.

LINGLEY. I would like firstly, therefore, to explain that my reason for calling this meeting is, if I may put it in this manner, to draw up a clean balance sheet.

DUKE. Quite.

LINGLEY. Now, secondly—if I may say so—

TOM. You may say anything you like, old boy, only for goodness' sake say it.

LINGLEY. Sir! I—

MRS. C-BANKS. Order, please. Order.

TOM. I'll have the same, with a splash.

LINGLEY. Oh, please don't all keep interrupting.

MRS. C-BANKS. Well, they always say "order" at meetings—

DUKE. Quite!

LINGLEY. Where was I?

DUKE. Drawing up a balance sheet.

TOM. "Laughter."

LINGLEY. And trying to explain my reason for doing so.

DUKE. Quite.

TOM. Quite *what?*

LINGLEY.   My reasons—

TOM.   *Have* you any?

LINGLEY.   (*Sits down in disgust.*)   I shall say no more.

TOM.   *Good.*

MRS. MIDGET.   Oh, sir, don't rob the gentleman of his amusement!   'E may not 'ave much more opportunity.

LINGLEY.   I only thought, in view of the shortness of time at our command, *and* the nature of the harbour we are rapidly approaching,—I shall therefore call on Mr. Duke for a few words.   He should, professionally, know more of the matter than we do.   Ahem!   The Rev. W. Duke, M. C.

DUKE (*without rising*).   All I can say is—if we *are* all dead then let us hope we have done our jobs to the best of our ability.

LINGLEY.   I've never been late for an appointment in my life.

DUKE.   And now that we're nearing this—this dread examiner, we think something should be done. And we've put off really thinking what to do till the last moment.   Naturally we *would*, we're all English.

MRS. C-BANKS. Rule Britannia!

DUKE. You ask for my professional advice! I have none to give. The steward himself has none to give.

MRS. MIDGET. You might pray for us, sir.

DUKE. I would if I thought my prayer would be worth anything. But now I don't understand. To pray for something one doesn't understand is to be an idolater.

MRS. MIDGET. Oh, we mustn't be one of those.

DUKE. It's the first time in my—it's the first *time* I've never known what to do. It's a strange business, this being dead. (*The drum is heard again.* ANN *and* HENRY *appear in the centre. A pause and then the* REV. MR. DUKE *notices the couple.*) Oh, come in. (ANN *and* HENRY *come in and stand away from the others.*) By the way. I suppose we're all agreed on that point?

LINGLEY. What point?

TOM. Ask these two.

LINGLEY. What point?

DUKE. *Are we all dead or are we not?*

LINGLEY. That's what I called this meeting to decide. (*To* ANN *and* HENRY.) You two, won't you sit down? (*No reply, they simply huddle closer together, and stand aloof left.*) No? No. Very well, then. The motion in front of us is, I think, perfectly plain to all. "Are we—" Who will speak first?

MRS. C-BANKS. I will. For I think it's a most impertinent question to be asked. If I am dead, why can't I be dead in private? Personally, I believe I *am* dead. My corsets have never fitted so comfortably anyway.

LINGLEY. Mr. Prior?

TOM. I *know*. And I don't care a damn one way or the other.

MRS. C-BANKS. The man's a plebiscite.

LINGLEY. Mr. Duke?

DUKE. Agreed. Mr. Lingley?

LINGLEY (*pause*). I agree. Mrs. Midget?

MRS. MIDGET. Ladies and gents, all I want to know is this, and I really don't know what's goin' on. But if it *'as* 'appened—it would greatly please me to know that I've been *done proper*.

LINGLEY. I beg your pardon.

MRS. MIDGET. You know, the street, the neighbours, the sherry wine and cake—and flowers.

LINGLEY.   This is beside the point—do you think you're dead or do you not?

MRS. MIDGET.   Oh, I leave it entirely to you, sir.

LINGLEY.   I take it in favour of the motion.   And now you two young people?

TOM.   They know.   They've always known.

LINGLEY.   Please, please, let them answer for themselves.   Well?   Well, what do you say?

HENRY.   We have nothing to say.

LINGLEY.   I suppose we must disregard your evidence.   As far as the rest of us are concerned, I think there is nothing more to be done than to enter the verdict that this board (*commences to write*) "certifies itself to be dead."   And the next thing for me to decide—is the most effective way— in all our interests—to meet and talk with this examiner.

TOM.   Do you mean we want to get out of it if we can?

LINGLEY.   If we can.   And—if we can't—we want to get out of it as lightly as we can.

MRS. C-BANKS.   Go on.

LINGLEY.   And we're under a great disadvantage. You see we do not know what sort of a person this examiner is, who is suddenly to pounce upon us. He is bound to be a hard, stern business man. In which case, I suggest I am the one best fitted to deal with him.

Tom.   Hear, hear!

Duke.   Supposing he isn't anything like that? Supposing he is something even *you* can't understand? Supposing he is really *the* examiner? Don't you think we all ought to speak for ourselves?—if we can.

Lingley.   It's if we *can't* I'm thinking of.

Duke.   I wish we knew. I certainly wish we knew.
(Scrubby *enters from behind bar.*)

Mrs. C-Banks.   Why not ask that steward person about him? They must have met before.

Tom.   Not a bad idea at all, Mrs. Cliveden-Banks.

Lingley.   The steward! Exactly, will someone go and fetch him?

Scrubby.   You want *me,* sir?

Lingley.   What the—!
Scrubby.   I have been here all the time.

Lingley.   But, we—

Scrubby. You wanted to ask me about the examiner, sir?

Lingley. Yes, if you would be so good.

Scrubby. What did you want to know exactly, sir?

Lingley. Well, he can't be tipped, that of course is obvious—but between ourselves—what sort of a person is he?

Scrubby. I can't say. I don't know. It all depends.

Lingley. Depends on what?

Scrubby. Yourselves, sir. I have seen some men and women before him cry for—but no, I can't say. (*He crosses right toward door centre.*)

Lingley. Tell us just this, Mr. Scrubby, what do you think we really ought to do—how exactly should we approach him?

Scrubby. I have been asked that question nearly five thousand times, sir; I have always answered that it is better to leave the approaching to him. (*Starts to go out centre.*)

Duke. Scrubby, have I any chance?

Scrubby (*standing in door silhouetted against the golden light outside*). You *all* have chances, sir.

Duke. What's he like?

Scrubby. He's the wind and the skies and the earth, sir. He knows the furthest eddy of the high tide up the remotest cove. He knows the simpleness of beauty and the evilest thoughts of the human mind. He'll know all your evil thoughts.

Duke (*quickly*). God!

Scrubby. Yes, sir, he will. (*Looks out on to the deck.*) Would you excuse me now, please? I can tell no more; and a seagull has just fallen on to the deck. I'm afraid it may have broken its wing. If so, I must try and mend it.

Ann. Poor thing!

Scrubby. Yes, madam, it's very sad the way the birds die in these strange waters. (*He walks off along the deck.*)

Duke. Just like the first day at school again.

Tom. *Now* do you want to deal with him—collectively? Or will you just make yourself responsible for your own sins?

Lingley. Oh, come, come, come! We mustn't all get jumpy. I still think we ought to be prepared though my own conscience is perfectly clear.

MRS. C-BANKS.   Then you'd better worry about *ours*, dear Mr. Lingley.   Come, tabulate us, as it were.

LINGLEY.   Excellent.   Then I can put all the cases before this—this examiner briefly and to the point.

MRS. C-BANKS.   It should save us a great amount of trouble.

LINGLEY.   So, if you will all just give me a few details about yourselves—and any special little reference you might like me to bring forward.   Mrs. Cliveden-Banks, let me start with you.   What shall I say about *you* to tl·is—er—examiner?

MRS. C-BANKS.   I should just say I am—or *was*—Mrs. Cliveden-Banks—and leave it at that.

LINGLEY.   Um!   Oh, very well; you, Mrs. Midget?

MRS. MIDGET.   Oh, I dunno.

LINGLEY.   Oh, dear, dear, dear!   Is that really all?

MRS. MIDGET.   Yes, please, sir.

LINGLEY.   All right—not at all satisfactory, but I suppose all right—in my hands.   I can answer for myself of course.   You, Mr. Prior?

Tom. Oh, say, I'm an old drunk. Or rather a young one.

Lingley. That won't help you very much.

Tom. How do *you* know?

Lingley. But you must have had some redeeming qualities that will help you? For instance, were you good to your mother or—did you go to Oxford?

Tom. Put down the truth—he will know it anyway.

Lingley. Really, you're none of you being very helpful. (*Writes.*) A drunk—er—a Mrs. Cliveden-Banks—er—and an I dunno.

Mrs. C-Banks. I should prefer to precede the drunk.

Lingley. Very well. (*To* Henry.) Now, sir, how *can* you assist me?

Henry. I can't.

Lingley. But—you then, madam?

Ann. He speaks for both of us.

Henry. We have nothing to say.

Lingley. It is really most discourteous of you! Mr. Duke, I can rely on *you* at any rate.

DUKE. You can rely on me for *one* piece of information.

LINGLEY. Thank you very much.

DUKE. I now entirely agree with Mr. Prior for calling you a pompous old idiot!

TOM. Cheers.

LINGLEY. What?—just because I'm trying to do my duty!

DUKE. Your duty! Your rubbish! You're doing what you are because you're in a blue funk! And I don't blame you. I'm in a blue funk, too! But not so much as to make an utter ass of myself by trying to get out of this with balance sheets and board meetings! You want to try and impress this examiner with your cleverness, your business importance, your supposed interest in your fellow creatures. You're hoping to save your own skin that way. And I think it's pretty rotten!

LINGLEY. Indeed. Destructive criticism is very simple. Then perhaps *you* can advise me.

DUKE. I can advise nothing.

LINGLEY. Um! That's *very* useful.

MRS. MIDGET. Oh, sir, not just *one* word of 'elp?

DUKE. That is different. If I can *help* I will.
But you mustn't take anything I say in the nature
of advice. The blind leading the blind, you know.
I can only tell you what I am going to do myself,
and I may be wrong.

TOM. *What* are you going to do, Duke? (*Staccato.*)

DUKE. I have been trying to look into myself
silently, trying to examine my past thoughtfully and
humbly——to seek out all the faults and not try to
excuse them. But to know all that I am responsible
for; and when I see my life, lying before me like a
blurred map, I am going to pray to be able to make
one more prayer. But for myself; I am not fit to
pray for others. If any of you care to do likewise
please do so if it will comfort you. Look back.

MRS. C-BANKS. I *could* look back, of course, but
I don't intend to. Remember Mrs. Lot.

MRS. MIDGET. Thank you, sir.

DUKE. No, no, now that's just what I didn't
want you to do. You see, Mrs. Midget——try to
understand——we're just shipmates, you and I——trying
to help one another. I'm not a captain any longer.
I cannot pray for others. Perhaps the realisation of
that is the beginning of my punishment. I've *lost*
my job.

LINGLEY.   I don't suppose it was worth much anyway.

DUKE.   It was the most glorious job in the world. I suppose a man never really knows he's incompetent until he's sacked, and I can't, I can't understand and I *ought* to.   It's my *job* to; and it's beastly hard *not* to be able to.   It's heartbreaking—it's— (*To* PRIOR.)   Give me a cigarette.

(*The siren is heard again.* HENRY *moves away from* ANN.)

LINGLEY.   Well, let's get down to hard facts—I suggest.

DUKE.   Too late.   Didn't you hear?

LINGLEY.   What?

ANN.   *I* heard.

TOM.   What?

DUKE.   The siren.

TOM (*after a pause suddenly hysterical*).   I didn't hear anything—I didn't hear anything.

(DUKE *and* TOM *rise.* TOM *in sudden panic.*)

DUKE.   Now, now, Prior.

TOM.   I didn't, I didn't! (*Another pause.*) But I can feel something though, can't you?

DUKE. No.

TOM. The boat's stopped.

DUKE. Exactly. We're in.

(*Another pause. The siren is repeated.*)

TOM. No, no! I won't face it! I daren't! It's all been bluff on my part! Let me get away! Let me get—!

DUKE (*rising with hand on* PRIOR). Prior, my boy!

TOM. I can't face it. I want to get away! Make the boat go on!

ANN. Henry! (*She gets closer to him.*)

TOM. Let me get away. (*Struggling to get away.*)

DUKE. We can none of us get away. We've stopped for good now. This is the judgment.

TOM (*pulling himself together*). No, it can't be. Here in the smoke-room of a liner?

DUKE. Why *shouldn't* it be here in the smoke-room of a liner? Have any of us really ever troubled very much to think where-and-how-and-when it might be?

ANN (*quietly*). Henry. They won't *separate* us —they *can't*.

[124]

(HENRY *merely holds her closer—as if in defiance.*)

DUKE.   We're for it now all right.

(DUKE *sits right of table with his face buried in his hands.*)

TOM.   We must stick together.   Duke, man, you *must* pray even if the words are meaningless. Don't desert duty at the last moment.   We're in the night and I want a prayer.   I want a prayer from a man, I don't care if he's a clergyman or not.

MRS. MIDGET (*going to* DUKE).   You *ought* to pray, your Reverence.

TOM.   Even if you can't understand what for— you understand *us.*

DUKE.   You really think I ought to, Mrs. Midget?

MRS. MIDGET (*bending over him*).   Yes, sir, pardon the liberty.   There's no 'arm in 'abits—if they're *good* 'abits; and prayer *is* a good 'abit.

DUKE (*without rising—but slowly facing front and with utter simplicity and sincerity*).   Forgive me then, for I don't know—"Gentle Jesus, meek and mild, look upon a little child—children—pardon our simplicity, suffer us to come to Thee.   God bless father and mother, Harriet (she was my nurse), all kind friends, make me a good boy.   Amen."   That was the first prayer I ever learnt, so it's probably the finest.   Say it to yourselves if you want to; and remember—Harriet—she was a worthy soul.

Ann (*after a long pause*).   Henry, let's hide. (*She takes his hand and they drift off together, left.*)

Mrs. Midget.   I feel better.

(Scrubby *enters from the left, giving a glance back as he does so.*)

Scrubby (*brightly—and business-like*).   We're in, ladies and gentlemen, we're in.

Duke.   Yes, yes, we know.

Scrubby.   The examiner is just coming on board. His cutter's alongside.   He'll *be* with you in a second.   (*He goes out on to the deck.*)

Duke.   We can do nothing now.

Mrs. C-Banks (*in a whisper*).   Mr. Lingley— Mr. Lingley!

Lingley.   Well?

Mrs. C-Banks.   Well—hadn't we better all stand up?   (*All rise.*)

Lingley.   Eh?   Oh, yes, of course, it would be more polite.

Duke.   Politeness!

Scrubby (*appearing and announcing*).   The Examiner.

Tom (*quickly and quietly appealingly*).   Duke!

Duke.   Quiet.

(The Rev. Frank Thomson *is heard shouting off, right.*)

Thomson.   Hello, hello, hello there, I say! Where is everyone?   Where are you, Duke? (*He appears in the centre.   An elderly and massive clergyman, rotund, rubicund and jovial.   He is dressed in white drill and a topee.   But he wears a clergyman's collar and black bib.*)   Ah, there you are!   Duke, my old boy, how are you?

Duke.   Good—!   My—!   Well—!   Well, I'm dashed if it isn't old "grease spot." (*Crossing and shaking hands.*)

Thomson.   It is, sir, and greasier than ever. Phew!   This climate!   Well, I am glad to see you after all this time.   How are you, Duke?   Have a good passage?   You're looking fit. (*Taking off topee and wiping forehead.*)

Duke.   I'm not *feeling* it.

Thomson.   I only heard this morning your boat was due in this afternoon.   I'd seen your name on the passenger list of course—so I hurried down especially to meet you, I'd been up country. (*Sits at table left.*)

DUKE.   Thank you.

THOMSON.   Well, how goes everything?   I'm bursting for news!   How's Fergusson—still in the same old place?

DUKE.   No, they've made him a bishop now.

THOMSON.   Good Lor', they *would*.   Well, I hope he likes it.   And what's become of Maltby; and that little fellow with the red hair and spectacles?   I never could remember his name.   (*Lights a cigarette.*)   And do you still go for your blow-out at Simpson's every pay day, you young rascal?   Tell me, what's the meat like there now?

DUKE (*greatly agitated and in no mood for* THOMSON's *frivolity*).   Thomson, I'm delighted to see you again, of course, and I'm dying to tell you everything afterwards—*if I can*—but can't you realise—at this moment—how terribly worried I am?

THOMSON.   Worried—worried about what?

DUKE.   This—this person.

THOMSON.   What person?

DUKE.   This person—or whoever it is—who's just coming to examine us.

Thomson. The examiner! Oh, I shouldn't worry about him!

Duke. What—do—you—mean?

Thomson. *I'm* the examiner!

(*General movement.*)

Duke. You—you are!

Thomson. Well, I'm one of 'em anyway. We've got dozens on the job. And they *will* shove all the duds on to it. My dear boy, our profession is not what it used to be. Terribly overcrowded, too, believe me.

Duke. You're—my—examiner?

Thomson. Yes—you're under *my* orders now. And I tell you, my boy, you'll have to mind your p's and q's; and *how* you'll have to slog at it! But I've fixed your "digs" up for you all right; they're not up to much, but clean, in the same house as myself; the old woman's quite a decent sort. And it's near your work, right in the centre of the parish, so you couldn't do better, really.

Duke. *Work?*

Thomson. I find it quite handy myself.

Duke. "Parish—slog at it." Thomson, Thomson, you don't mean I haven't lost my job after all? Don't torture me, tell me quickly.

THOMSON. Of course you haven't lost it. You haven't started it yet. You're just beginning it.

DUKE. Not lost my job? Still got my job. Oh, thank you! Oh, thank God! I will work harder now every moment, I swear I will, Mr. Thomson. Harder than ever! Oh, do you all hear? My job I was so keen on—it's not been taken from me after all. My—oh! (*sits at table, left, and quietly cries*) —job.

THOMSON (*patting him on shoulder*). There, there, boy, there, there! Whatever made you think it would be taken from you? (DUKE *sobs*.) There, there, it's quite all right.

MRS. C-BANKS (*at back on the seat with LING-LEY*). I'm very glad to see they know each other so well—but what about us?

LINGLEY. This might be a suitable moment to approach him.

MRS. C-BANKS. Try.

LINGLEY. I will. (*Importantly crossing to examiner who takes no notice.*) Sir—ahem—my name is Lingley—of Ling—

THOMSON. Go away.

LINGLEY. I have advocated myself—or rather my fellow passengers have advocated me—their spokesman as it were—

THOMSON (*still attending to* DUKE).   Go away.

LINGLEY.   And I thought this might be a good moment to approach a somewhat—

THOMSON (*turning on him positively*).   Will you go away, sir?

LINGLEY.   Certainly. (*Retires.*)   I've no wish to stay where I'm not wanted. (*Goes back to his seat.*)

MRS. C-BANKS.   How very rude!

LINGLEY.   I don't believe he's the examiner at all.

MRS. C-BANKS.   Of course, Mr. Duke will get off lightly. (*Rises.*)   A friend at court, you see. Influence! Ah! It's always the same. Shall *I* say something to him?

LINGLEY.   Good Lor', madam, *no*.

THOMSON (*to* DUKE).   Feeling better now?

DUKE.   I'm very sorry, sir.   But it means such a lot to me.   You understand.

THOMSON.   Perfectly.   I had exactly the same feeling when it happened to *me*.   But you've nothing to worry about except your work.

DUKE.   I'm full of energy.

Thomson. Then you can start your apprentice-ship now and help me with this bunch. By the way, there aren't many of you.

Duke. No, sir.

Thomson. Then it won't take long and we can get on shore for dinner.

Lingley. Sir, if I find my trial's being "scamped" I shall appeal.

Thomson (*to* Scrubby). Take that man away, will you?

Scrubby. Certainly, sir. This way, Mr. Lingley.

Lingley (*as he goes out centre*). It's disgraceful.

Thomson. And the rest had better wait *with* him—outside.

Scrubby. Very good, sir. Will you all come this way, please?

Mrs. C-Banks (*making a large sweep towards* Thomson). How do you do? (*Seeing she is ig-nored she follows the others out.*) Oh!

(Tom *goes out, centre, followed by* Mrs. Midget.)

Thomson. That's all. (Scrubby *follows them off.*) Now, we'll get to work.

Duke. Yes, sir.

[132]

THOMSON. Let's see; who have we got on board? (*Reads from his note-book.*) Cliveden-Banks, Midget, Prior and the officious gent who spoke to me—yourself.

DUKE. There's an awfully nice quiet young couple.

THOMSON. Oh? I don't remember them. They're not on the passenger list. We'll begin with the officious one. (*Calls.*) Scrubby! Where's that fellow got to?

SCRUBBY (*appearing*). Here, sir.

THOMSON. Oh. (*Reading.*) Show in Mr. Lingley.

SCRUBBY (*calling off centre*). Mr. Lingley!

(LINGLEY *appears at door centre.*)

THOMSON. Come in. Sit down. There.

(LINGLEY *sits in chair at table right.*)

LINGLEY (*rather truculently*). Well?

THOMSON. Well, sir?

LINGLEY. I am Lingley, of Lingley, Limited.

THOMSON. Never mind the "Limited." You are just Lingley now.

LINGLEY. What am I charged with, anyway?

[133]

THOMSON.   With just being yourself.

LINGLEY.   I am very proud of being myself. From small beginnings I have worked up to great things.   I have never hesitated but have always kept to the straight path.

THOMSON.   I know.   But *how?*

LINGLEY.   By hard work—enterprise!

THOMSON.   Enterprise!   Dishonesty.

LINGLEY (*hotly*).   That's a lie!

THOMSON.   Very well.   Your case is over.   Get out.

LINGLEY.   (*Rises, hesitates.*)   Just a minute. Let's talk this over.

THOMSON.   Well?   Is it a lie—or is it the truth?

LINGLEY.   I—I'm afraid you don't understand *business*.

THOMSON.   Not the way *you* conduct it.   Why, you've been a rascal from the very start.   You commenced your career by breaking a playmate's head against a granite curb because he had a painted tin horse.   You wanted to get it.

LINGLEY.   Well, I got it.

THOMSON.   Oh, I grant you that!   That's how

[134]

you've made that glorious straight path you boast about. By knocking down anyone who came across it or tried to turn you off it. The foundation of Lingley, Limited, was laid when you stole the plans of a turbine engine—and let the inventor die in poverty.

LINGLEY. I've not been wicked. People respect me.

THOMSON. Do they? To your face, perhaps. Some men get found out during their lives, Lingley. You are only found out now. Come; off you get.

(HENRY *and* ANN *appear at the centre door coming from left. They hesitate, looking in for a second, as* if awaiting their turn, then pass on right. DUKE *sees them.*)

LINGLEY. I—I—

THOMSON. There is no appeal. You will suffer as you made others suffer. (*Pause.*)

(THOMSON'S *manner is not hard and vindictive. He is kindly, tolerant and possibly even reluctant to dole out justice. But he is firm and just.*)

LINGLEY (*after a pause*). Give me a second chance.

THOMSON. Did *you* give anybody a second

[135]

chance? No, you must learn, my son. (*He turns and makes a note in his book.*)

(LINGLEY *looks defiantly for a moment at* THOM-SON, *whose back is turned, as if he'd like to strike him.*)

THOMSON (*turning. Quietly*). That's all.

(LINGLEY *slowly turns and goes out centre to left, utterly broken and dejected.*)

DUKE. Thomson!

THOMSON. Don't look so shocked. It must be done. Suffering sometimes works wonderful trans-formations. Let's hope, boy, let's hope. Scrubby!

SCRUBBY. Sir.

THOMSON (*to* SCRUBBY). Just see he goes the right way.

SCRUBBY. Very good, sir.

(*He follows* LINGLEY.)

DUKE (*rises*). I wish you'd see the young couple next. I know *they* must be suffering.

THOMSON. What young couple is this?

DUKE. I told you about them.

THOMSON. Yes, but I've had no information from any other quarter. It's funny.

DUKE. They seem so devoted. You'll have a pleasant job with them, I know.

THOMSON. But who exactly are they?

DUKE. Well, I used to call them, to myself, "the lovers."

(SCRUBBY *has appeared again in the centre.*)

THOMSON. Steward, do you know anything about a young couple on this boat?

SCRUBBY. Oh, those two, sir! You wouldn't want to see them.

DUKE. Not see them?

THOMSON. Why *shouldn't* I want to see them?

SCRUBBY. They're "half-ways," sir.

THOMSON. Half-ways. Oh, that explains it. No, it wouldn't be much use my seeing them. Show in—Mrs. Cliveden-Banks.

SCRUBBY. Yes, sir. (*He goes out left.*)

DUKE. You're not even going to see them?

THOMSON. I *can't,* old boy.

DUKE (*curiously*). What is a "half-way," Thomson?

[137]

Thomson. You'll learn, Duke, you'll learn in good time.

Duke. But I wish you would—

(Scrubby *appears again announcing.*)

Scrubby. Mrs. Cliveden-Banks!

(*She enters left and gushingly crosses to* Thomson. Scrubby *goes.*)

Mrs. C-Banks. How do you do? How *do* you do? *Very* pleased to meet you.

Thomson. Delighted to meet you, Mrs. Cliveden-Banks. Come and sit down.

Mrs. C-Banks. Thank you. Very sultry weather for the time of the year, isn't it? Still, we've had a lovely passage, haven't we, *dear* Mr. Duke?

Duke. Oh, yes, delightful, *dear* Mrs. Cliveden-Banks.

(Mrs. Cliveden-Banks *sits where Lingley sat.*)

Thomson. I'm glad you enjoyed yourself.

Mrs. C-Banks. Oh, I did, I did. Thanks to your kind friend, Mr. Duke. We clung together like limpets. I really don't know *what* I should have done without him. What wonderful men our church turns out, Mr—er

[138]

THOMSON.   Thomson, madam.

MRS. C-BANKS.   No; surely not one of the *Berkshire* Thomsons?

THOMSON.   Not that I am aware of.

MRS. C-BANKS.   Ah! a pity.   My great-great-grandfather was a Berkshire Thomson.

THOMSON.   Really?   My great-great-grandfather was hanged for horse-thieving.

MRS. C-BANKS.   How quaint.

THOMSON.   Mrs. Cliveden-Banks—

MRS. C-BANKS.   Do you play golf?

THOMSON.   I play indifferently.

MRS. C-BANKS.   I think all men ought to play golf.   It keeps them away from home such a lot. My husband, Colonel Cliveden-Banks, is quite an expert, I believe.

THOMSON.   Oh, yes, Bunny's hot stuff.   I was having a round with him not long ago.

MRS. C-BANKS.   I'm so glad to hear it.   (*A pause, then suddenly.*)   *What* did you say?   You had a round with my husband not long ago?

THOMSON.   He was in terrific form.

Mrs. C-Banks (*alarmed*).   When was this?

Thomson.   Oh, about a week ago, I think.

Mrs. C-Banks.   But I don't understand. Is he *here?*

Thomson.   He's waiting for you.   (*Rises.*)
Yes, we had a great game.   He'll tell you all about
it when you land.

Mrs. C-Banks.   I *don't land!*——How did *he* get
here?

Thomson.   Poor old Bunny died a couple of
months ago.

Mrs. C-Banks.   How wicked of him.   He might
have let me know.

Thomson.   Perhaps he didn't think you'd care
very much one way or the other.

Mrs. C-Banks.   Why not?   There was life in-
surance——how like him, how very like him.   Always
self-centred.   Look at the passage money I've wasted.
(*Suddenly.*)   Benjamin and I are *both* dead then?

Thomson.   Quite dead.

Mrs. C-Banks (*hopefully*).   That makes the
marriage null and void.

Thomson.   Your marriage is only just beginning.

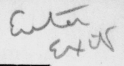

MRS. C-BANKS. How droll you are. But how nice of you to put it that way.

THOMSON. Now will you go ashore? You'll find everything most comfortable. A villa, servants, all you want—and your husband waiting—with outstretched arms.

MRS. C-BANKS. Yes, I can see him; exactly like a monkey.

THOMSON. I hope you will be able to see his *heart*. I know it's aching for you very badly.

MRS. C-BANKS. How ghastly.

THOMSON. What's the matter?

MRS. C-BANKS. What *right's* he got to bob up again like this?

THOMSON. Every right, and we're very glad to have him here. Your husband is a very useful man.

MRS. C-BANKS. How well I know that phrase! It has always been used of Benjamin in every new office he's undertaken, at the start. Later he invariably got the push.

(HENRY *and* ANN *pass the centre door again during this speech, look anxiously in and then pass on left.*)

THOMSON. And do you know why? Because of his wife's malicious tongue.

[141]

Mrs. C-Banks (*rises, crosses left*). How dare you? I'm sure I've never said anything bad about Benjamin. I don't know that I've said anything good about him, because there's nothing good *to* say about him. (*Sits.*)

Thomson. There is a very great deal of good in Bunny. But it was always stifled back by you. He was a staunch, a devoted husband—look what he gave *you*—and what did you give in return? Nothing!

Mrs. C-Banks. But I haven't seen him for years.

Thomson. It was *your* neglect—not his.

Mrs. C-Banks. Oh, but he looks so funny.

Thomson. The only funny thing about him is that he wants to see you. Why he should *want* to see you is beyond me. But he does, and he's going to.

Mrs. C-Banks. And what shall I be exactly?

Thomson. You'll be his wife; and in time you will learn to be a *good* wife.

Mrs. C-Banks. I refuse absolutely.

Thomson. You *can't* refuse. (*With finality.*)

[142]

(*A long pause.*)

MRS. C-BANKS.   I won't do it! I won't, I won't.

DUKE.   Why won't you, Mrs. Cliveden-Banks?

MRS. C-BANKS.   *He* knows—ask him. (*Indicating* THOMSON.)

DUKE.   Mr. Thomson—?

(THOMSON *is silent, waiting.*)

MRS. C-BANKS (*to* THOMSON).   You know as well as I do, it's his eyes. The look in his eyes. You know I couldn't face them any more—

THOMSON.   Yes;—you never could look him in the eyes. You're a thoroughly bad lot. You trapped him; you were grasping, you made him marry you. You—you—you—

MRS. C-BANKS.   Don't let me down before *him.* (*Indicating* DUKE.)

THOMSON.   I wouldn't if you'd been a *good* harlot; but you weren't, you were a bad one.

MRS. C-BANKS.   (*Pause.*)   Rather a vulgar way of putting it!

DUKE.   Dear, dear, only a poor unfortunate after all.

[143]

Thomson. No, Duke, *not* a poor unfortunate. This old woman was once a beautiful young girl, outwardly, but she was never an unfortunate, never. She's been just a schemer. And somehow she's always managed to fall on her feet. There were two other men before she met Cliveden-Banks, richer men too than he was then. But she saw something *steady* in Bunny, so she made him marry her. He found out all about it later—and he's never told her. Too unselfish—too "big"—too loyal.—So she goes back to him. I hope he *beats* her—but I know he won't. Anyway, she'll get her punishment. The eyes that made her run away.—Only remember, Mrs. Cliveden-Banks, it won't be Bunny who'll know now, it will be you and I and everybody *except* Bunny. He'll have forgotten. (*Over to left of table.*)

Mrs. C-Banks. Um! Now let me see. A villa —servants. And you really think Benjamin would idealise me? Oh, well, I suppose it might be worse. I'll go.

Thomson. Of *course* you will.

Mrs. C-Banks. For his sake, yes. I see it's my duty to. Ah, duty, duty, such a compelling thing. Speaking of duties, there are no *customs,* I suppose? No. Good. Perhaps you'll both come and dine with the Colonel and me—one night. Goodbye,

[144]

Mr.—(*moves up centre to door*)—er—Tomkins. (*Pause.*) You swine.

(She goes out.)

THOMSON.   Phew! this place wants fumigating.

DUKE.   Thomson—what *are* "half-ways"?

(Before THOMSON *can reply* PRIOR *enters left excitedly.)*

TOM.   Duke—Duke!

DUNE.   Yes.   (*Crosses left.*)

TOM.   Make him see *me* next.

DUKE.   Really, Prior—

TOM.   You must, I can't stand the suspense. My nerves aren't right—and I can't stand it.

DUKE.   There's nothing to worry about.

TOM (*shouts*). I tell you I can't stand it. I want to be put out.

THOMSON (*turning and coming down*). What's the matter, boy?

TOM.   Oh, sir, if you please, I want you to deal with me next. It isn't fair treating me like the others —I'm very highly strung.

THOMSON.   Come in, boy, come in and don't be frightened. (*Passes* TOM *to chair at table right.*)

[145]

We're not going to hurt you. (*Leading him over.*) There, sit down there. Now, what's the trouble?

TOM. I want to be dealt with, sir. I want to *know*.

THOMSON. Calm yourself, boy, calm yourself. (*Giving him glass.*) Drink this. You're fond of your drink, I know.

TOM. Thanks, sir. (*Drinks and then holds out glass again.*)

THOMSON. Well, what do you want? (*Goes right of table and sits.*)

TOM. I want to be killed—I want to be killed.

THOMSON. Um! Healthy outlook you've got, haven't you?

TOM. No, I haven't. I'm a weak character. I want to be let off lightly. I want to be hit over the head with a stone and finished.

THOMSON. Duke, send ashore for a bag of stones, will you?

TOM. Oh, don't joke! I'll drop all sarcasm— it's the only thing that kept me going up till now— but I'll drop it now if you will.

THOMSON. Certainly.

Tom.   I know—at least I guess what you're doing with the others.   You're keeping them going, keeping them going with punishment and promises and things.   Well, *I* don't want to be kept going.   I want blank.

Thomson.   Impossible.

Tom.   But I'm dead.   (*Rises.*)   And I demand the right to be properly dead.   I've always dreamt about being dead—when I've slept at all.

Thomson.   How old are you?

Tom (*sits*).   Oh, hundreds of years—I must be. Give me blank.

Thomson.   You're going on like the others. You've got to.

Tom.   I won't, I won't!

Thomson.   You'll find it quite easy to forget here, you know.

Tom.   Easy to forget what?   You're not suggesting I'm to go on, and without *this?*   (*The glass.*)

(Mrs. Midget *appears centre.*)

Thomson.   Yes.

Tom.   Is that all I'm to forget?

Thomson.   Yes.

[147]

Tom. As if I could! As if I would anyway.
You damned torturer. I see what you want me to
do. You want me to chuck drink, develop a nice
clean brain and remember all the other horrors! No,
I won't do it. It's all I've got, it's my only comfort
and if I'm to go on I won't give it up. See? But
I'm not going to go on. Kill me! There, it's not
asking much. And look at all the trouble it will
spare you. I'm not worth saving. I'm not really.

Thomson. You've suffered.

Tom. Ha! (*As if to say "Haven't I?"*)

Thomson. Can't I do *anything?*

Tom. No, you can't.

Mrs. Midget (*quietly from the back*). Perhaps
I could, sir.

Thomson (*facing sharply*). What do you want?

Mrs. Midget. My name's Midget, sir. Excuse
me bargin' in as it were, but—

Thomson. I'm very pleased to meet you—yes,
yes, I know all about you. But you've no business
here yet.

Mrs. Midget. Oh, but I *have*. You see, yer
Reverence, when I first got on to this big boat nobody
would speak to me. I was lost as it were—was—

[148]

and then young Mr. Prior was very kind to me. '*E* spoke to me and broke the icicles, as is said, and if he is in trouble I really don't feel I could put my 'ead on my pillow to-night—if I 'ave one—after what 'e done for me. (*Goes to* Tom, *touches him.*) Now what is all this fluster and to do, anyway? It's about the booze, ain't it?

Tom.   Booze—eh? Oh, well—yes—drink *is* certainly mixed up with it.

Mrs. Midget.   Nasty 'orrid stuff.

Tom.   Beautiful stuff, Mrs. Midget.

Mrs. Midget.   Mind you I don't say there's any 'arm in a man 'aving 'is beer if he wants 'is beer, but the man I does object to is the man who's *always* wanting it. I shouldn't think you've ever 'ad much of a *chance,* though, 'ave you, sir?

Tom.   I've had every chance, Mrs. Midget. I was spoilt. I was ungrateful. I ruined— Please drop it.

Mrs. Midget (*pause*).   There was a girl, too, wasn't there?

Tom.   Be quiet.

Mrs. Midget (*another pause*).   There *was* a girl, though, wasn't there?

[149]

Tom. Oh, yes, there was. How did you know?

Mrs. Midget. She was the final old 'ow do you do, I take it?

Tom. As you so poetically express it, she *was*.

(Henry *and* Ann *appear at door centre and unseen by the others stand listening apprehensively.*)

Mrs. Midget. She chucked you, didn't she? But you'll be different now. I know something about girls and—your Reverence (*behind* Tom *to* Thomson), I daresay this particular one might come along here some day?

Thomson. It's quite possible. But it doesn't always follow, Mrs. Midget, that just because a boy and girl are sweethearts, they may always go on together here. On the contrary, they're sometimes *separated*—so much depends—so much depends.

(Ann *utters a faint wail and* Henry *leads her further back into the shadows up left where they remain enviously watching the rest of the scene.* Mrs. Midget *looks sympathetically at* Henry *and*

Ann, *then resumes to* Tom.)

Mrs. Midget. What a triumph it would be for you if *your* girl suddenly appeared 'ere and found you—mind yer, it *might* 'appen—settled down and smart and respectable like, with a good job and a decent salary reg'lar every Saturday. (*To* Thomson.) I suppose you've got jobs 'ere, 'aven't you?

Thomson.   Plenty.

Mrs. Midget.   Now what you want is a nice, good, honest, steady respectable housekeeper who'd take care of you.

Tom (*annoyed*). Mrs. Midget—!

Mrs. Midget.   Yes, *she* might do.   Then all your things would be properly looked after.   With everything mended and darned ready for yer to put on. Someone to see yer didn't sit up too late, too often. No fussing mind, and call you in the morning with a nice 'ot cup of tea.   What time do you get up?

Tom.   Oh, don't!

Mrs. Midget.   Oh, you can 'ave your drinks, as long as you don't let them interfere with your meals or take away your appetite.   I'm a good cook I am, and if you left anything untouched it would upset me awful.

Thomson.   Mrs. Midget, you're suggesting.

Mrs. Midget.   I was *thinking* of it, yes.

Thomson.   Very fine, very fine of you.   There's a little cottage waiting for you, with a garden by the sea.

MRS. MIDGET (*enthusiastic*). There we *are* then!
The very spot. (*Sudden change to the practical.*)
'As it got a good sink?

THOMSON. You don't quite follow. True, Mr.
Prior is free to do as he chooses but he has not yet
arrived on the same plane as you have. He would
not be allowed to live there to begin with anyway.

MRS. MIDGET. Then why can't I go where *he's*
going? That's simple enough.

THOMSON. It would mean going back to the
slums.

MRS. MIDGET. And what's the matter with the
slums? They're all right.

TOM. I won't listen to the idea.

MRS. MIDGET (*pleading*). You can always give
me a week's notice.

TOM. I'm not worth bothering about.

MRS. MIDGET. I'm willing to 'ave a shot.

TOM. I can't understand this extraordinary interest anyway.

MRS. MIDGET. One good turn deserves another.
Sir, wouldn't the people who spoilt you be glad if
they knew you was in capable 'ands?

TOM.   They would be, I suppose.

MRS. MIDGET.   *And* doing well? (*With growing fervour.*)

TOM.   Er—yes—of course.

MRS. MIDGET.   That might ease those 'orrid thoughts of yours a bit too, mightn't it?

TOM.   It might.

MRS. MIDGET.   Well then, ain't it worth it, sir?

TOM.   Please don't keep on calling me "sir." I'm not a gentleman really.

MRS. MIDGET.   Aren't you, sir?

TOM.   No, I'm not. If I were, I shouldn't be hesitating as I am. Mr. Examiner, help me. *You* must be experienced in making decisions.

THOMSON.   No, boy, I can't help you in this. It's your own choice.

TOM.   Duke, I—

DUKE.   You know what Mr. Thomson said, it's for you to speak.

TOM.   Very well then. (*Pause.*) I'll go. (*Rising. Another Pause.*) By myself!

DUKE.   Prior!

TOM. *I'm not worth bothering about.*

THOMSON. And in those very words you've proved you are! Because you really meant 'em. Humility, my boy, humility! Take him away, Mrs. What's—er—name and do the best you can with him.

TOM. Mind you, I won't promise—I won't promise to be good.

MRS. MIDGET. No, sir, we'll just 'ope—mutual like.

TOM (*fingering his glass*). It's going to be difficult—yes, it's going to be difficult.

THOMSON. *That's* the way.

TOM. Thanks awfully. (*Sets down glass.*) And I will try.

(*He goes out on to the deck and off right.* MRS. MIDGET *overjoyed starts to follow him.*)

THOMSON. Good day, Mrs. Prior—you're a good mother.

MRS. MIDGET (*turning on* THOMSON *ferociously*). Blast you, how did you find out? Blast you! (*Then suddenly changing to pleading pitifully.*) You'll never tell 'im, will you? Promise you'll never let him know.

THOMSON.   I promise.

MRS. MIDGET (*going to* DUKE *and clutching him*). And you too, sir?

DUKE.   I promise, of course.

MRS. MIDGET (*turning back*). Thank you, both. You see he mustn't even guess. Oh, sirs, ain't it wonderful? He doesn't know me, and I've got him to look after at last—— Without any fear of me disgracing him, it's 'Eaven, that's what it is, it's 'Eaven!

TOM (*off*). Mrs. Midget.

MRS. MIDGET.   He wants me at last—yes, dearie, I'm coming. (*She goes out centre in ecstasy, and off right.*)

(THOMSON *and* DUKE *watch her off, then with a pleased chuckle,* THOMSON *picks up his hat and goes up to door centre.*)

THOMSON.   Come along, Duke. (*Starts out door.*)

(DUKE *follows but hesitates as he sees* HENRY *and* ANN *who have drawn up toward door, mystified, fearful and appealing, as if to say, "What about us"?* DUKE *looks at them sympathetically and stops* THOMSON, *calling his attention to them.*)

Duke.   Thomson, can't you?

Thomson (*coming back a step*).   Oh—is this the—young couple?

Duke.   Yes, sir.   Can't you?

(*Henry and Ann stand silently appealing.*)

Thomson.   (*Gazes at them thoughtfully then shakes his head as if regretfully, and most tenderly.*) Not *yet*, my children.

(Thomson *goes out, followed by* Duke.   Henry *and* Ann *stand hopeless and bewildered, they look from one to the other curiously; then she, terror-stricken in awful apprehension of the uncertainty of their plight, at their being ignored, at the mystery of it all, suddenly clutches* Henry's *arm and holds to him tightly.*)

CURTAIN

Scene II

The scene is now as it was before, the small table which was used for the meeting having been removed. It is moonlight outside. The moonlight pours in through the portholes and through the centre door which is wide open.

SCRUBBY *enters from the left. He collects a few glasses, and places them on a tray. He is tidying up. He then goes through the door behind the bar. Once more the mysterious drum is heard, and* ANN *appears from the deck.*

ANN. Henry! (*Goes to left.*) Henry! Henry, where are you? I want you! (*Up again.*) Henry! Henry! (*Left.*)

HENRY. (*From centre opening.*) Yes, dear?

ANN. Where have you been?

HENRY. Looking at the sea—

ANN. You know we've sailed again.

HENRY. Yes.

ANN. Why have we both been left behind?

HENRY. I don't know, dear. But what does it matter, we've been left together.

[157]

Ann.   Yes, you and I.

Henry.   The lights of that place have gone now. (*At porthole.*)

Ann (*up to* Henry *up centre*).   Where were you just now?   Where were you?

Henry.   Looking at the sea.

Ann (*arm in arm down centre*).   I've taken a dislike to the sea, husband.   It seems to me we should keep terribly close.

Henry.   Why, dear?

Ann.   Can't you ever feel when things are passing over you?   Bad things, I can.   They're round us now, all round.   They've been round us since we left that harbour.

Henry.   Why weren't *we* judged?

Ann.   I don't know—and I don't know why you left me for a while.   (*Sits.*)

Henry.   I thought I heard a dog bark.   It was Jock.   What's that?

Ann.   What?

Henry.   Something seemed to touch my hand. (*He is uneasy.*)   We should have insisted on being heard, we were cowards.

ANN.   Not because we are ashamed of our love.

HENRY.   No.   Because we were afraid of being separated.

ANN.   Yes.

(*A faint, very faint, sound of breaking glass off right.*)

HENRY (*pause—listens*).   It's strange, that tinkling noise like glass—sharp pieces of glass falling on stone.   Do you hear it, Ann?

ANN.   No, dear.

HENRY.   My nerves are all on edge.   I'd have sworn I did.   Ann, where are we going to?

ANN.   I can't think.   (*Rises, pause.*)   Perhaps it's the dreadful house with the double staircase in the hall, you know.

HENRY.   The stairs I run up and down trying to find you.

ANN.   Perhaps it isn't a dream place at all.

HENRY.   And since we left that harbour I feel we are bound for some dimly remembered place. . . . Ann, I feel—a breeze like a breath of new— of different air.

ANN.   They didn't question us.   Perhaps it's freedom.

HENRY.   Ann, Ann, wife, wife.   Don't let's get away from each other.   We don't know where we are, we don't know what's becoming of us, or where we're going.

ANN.   I don't really care what's becoming of me as long as I am with my husband.   What else matters?   But if *you* went away from me—

HENRY.   It seems you're rather leaning on me now!

ANN.   Shares, Henry.

HENRY.   Shares, Ann.

ANN.   You see, I love you.   I love you so much. I love the way you walk, the way you hold your head.   I love *you*.   I love your mouth.   (ANN *sits down.*   HENRY *kneels with arm round her.*)

HENRY.   My wonderful Ann.   They won't separate us now, will they, Ann?   Nothing can take one from the other now?

ANN.   Nothing—nothing.

HENRY.   Keep close though, keep close . . . Are *you* cold?

ANN (*takes hold of him*).   No.   I've got you, darling, I've got you.

HENRY.   Never let go.

[160]

Ann. Why aren't we closer? I thought we *would* be when we're dead.

Henry. I thought there would be no need for speech. That *we*, the *real* you and I would drift away together. Where is the utter completeness?— Oh, Ann—Ann—

Ann. Supposing, after all, we were wrong.

Henry. Wrong?—how wrong? What was that? (*Rises.*)

Ann. Just supposing—

Henry. Ann— (*Listening.*)

(Scrubby *comes in quickly. He puts down the empty tray on bar.*)

Scrubby. Good evening, madam, good evening, sir. (*Goes left.*)

Ann. Good evening, Scrubby.

Henry. Ann!!

Ann. Yes, dear?

Henry. There's Jock barking. (*Stepping right a pace.*)

Ann. Don't be silly.

Scrubby. Who's Jock, ma'am?

[161]

ANN. Our dog—at home.

HENRY. Listen! Listen! (*Stepping further right.*)

ANN. Don't be silly, Henry.

HENRY. I'd like *him* to be with us. Jock!

SCRUBBY. Keep close to him, miss, if you'll take my advice.

HENRY. You can tell us, you can help, can't you? Where are we going to?

SCRUBBY. We just go on like this, sir—forwards and backwards—backwards and forwards.

HENRY. For ever?

ANN. Alone?

SCRUBBY. Yes, quite alone. Until—

HENRY (*slightly excited*). Until what? Why is this happening to us?

SCRUBBY. It happens to all half-ways like—like we are.

ANN. But what are we, Scrubby? We—we half-ways?

SCRUBBY. We're the people who ought to have had more courage.

ANN. For what?

SCRUBBY.   To face life.

ANN.   Do you remember how you became a half-way?

SCRUBBY.   Oh, no.   I've been allowed to forget. I hope you'll be allowed to forget.   It would be too cruel if they didn't let you forget in time that you killed yourselves.

ANN.   Scrubby!   (*A pause—rises.*)

HENRY.   (*Cries out*).   My God! *that's* it!   Now I remember!   Suicide!

SCRUBBY.   Keep closer to him, madam.

HENRY.   The people who ought to have had more courage!   I see.   *That's* what we've done that wasn't right.

ANN.   Henry!   (*Goes to him.*)

HENRY.   The little bits are fitting together.

ANN.   Dear, don't worry.

HENRY.   Ann, I wanted to forget.   (*Collapses on chair above table.*)   Oh, don't say the damned torture's going to start all over again.   We'd reached the end of our tether as it was.   Ann—

ANN.   I'm with you still.   (*She stands behind his chair and puts her arms round him.*)

[163]

HENRY. But you can't face it, Ann, you can't stand it any more. I won't let you suffer—not another second. We'll kill ourselves, dear, and forget in each other's arms. Then we'll be so happy, sweet, so happy for ever. (*Pause.*) Oh, but it's over. We *have* killed ourselves. And we're *not* happy.

ANN. No—we're not. (*Sits down.*)

HENRY. We can't stand it, Ann.

ANN (*after a pause.*) We've got to.

SCRUBBY. Why did you kill yourselves?

ANN (*pause*). We weren't married, Scrubby.

SCRUBBY. Weren't you, madam? Oh, you two poor dears. Pardon my familiarity.

HENRY. I was trapped into a marriage.

ANN. He's so guileless, Scrubby.

HENRY (*indicating* ANN). Ann came to me in such a wonderful way. It was like dawn.

ANN. They'd been so cruel to him, Scrubby. Never an atom of love in his whole life before, was there, Henry?

HENRY. Never. Ann was the only true and good thing I've ever met. We loved. We loved. I gave my soul for love as Ann gave hers. We got

[164]

so *near* each other that we *knew* that there was only one minute spiritual barrier between us, and that we believed was Death.   Death can unify utterly.   We believed that—and yet we are just as if we had never died.

SCRUBBY.   You killed *yourselves*.

ANN.   We should have waited?

SCRUBBY.   Yes.

ANN.   Oh, Scrubby—you don't know the agony we've been through.   The way people talked—the things they said.

HENRY.   Lies—such bloody lies!   (*Rises.*)

ANN.   They smeared our love—smeared—

HENRY.   With their dirty tongues.

ANN.   You see, Scrubby, we didn't conceal it— we didn't pretend.

HENRY.   We weren't ashamed.   We started so proudly, so proudly.

ANN.   Till we were beaten down so bruised, so hurt.

HENRY.   But we should have gone on?

ANN.   Yes.

[165]

Scrubby. And now you children are faced with memories.

Henry. I remember the long sweep into the dark. The last thing I saw was Jock's face against the window. I can see him now—almost feel him—Jock! (*Stooping as if to pet the dog.*) Jock!

Scrubby. *Outside* the window, sir?

Henry. Yes—outside. (*To* Ann.) And then you, Ann—I haven't taken care of you well enough, and I've been a coward. (Ann *rises.*) Oh! to be given back even a little while—to try again. Our future here isn't Hell, it isn't Heaven, it's past imagination.

Scrubby. Eternity.

Henry. Ann, Ann, I must save you. I promise that I will. I'm the man. Oh, it's my fault, it's all my fault. We didn't understand, dear, that we should have been true and brave and fearless. Then nothing could have hurt us wherever we were, whatever we have been, or may be.

Ann. It's too late now.

Henry (*moving away*). Let me think, dear. There must be a way out. Let me think. The air seems fresher out here.

(*Walks slowly to the deck and leans over rail. After*

*a few seconds during the following dialogue, walks
slowly up and down, passing and re-passing the
entrance.   Gradually a bigger pause between each
pass till he doesn't come past.)*

Scrubby (*below settee*).   Don't let him go too
far, madam.   Call him now.

Ann.   Henry!

Henry.   Ann!

Ann.   Don't go too far away.

Henry (*off*).   No, dear!

Ann (*crosses to* Scrubby).   Why aren't people
kinder to each other, Scrubby?

Scrubby (Ann *sits left*).   Being unkind comes
more natural to most people, I'm afraid.

Ann.   I'd try to be kinder if I had it over again.
How sad there's no one left here to be kind to.

Scrubby (*crosses right to table*).   Present company excepted.   What did you like best in life?

Ann.   I liked so many things.   I loved the earth,
the scent of the earth, of newly cut grass, after rain;
and the trees, and all clear things like water.   Are
you very lonely, Scrubby?

Scrubby.   Oh no, ma'am, not on the whole.
I've all sorts of comforting little thoughts locked up

[167]

in my brain, so when I get a bit monotonous I just turn the key and out come the thoughts to dance in front of me. Very whimsical and entertaining some of them are, too, I must say.

ANN. I do hope we'll get on together. When I was living I did want people to look after, but I had so few friends. Now I've none excepting you.

SCRUBBY. You'll find lots of new friends, ma'am. Not quite the same, but most consoling. The birds come on board occasionally—and the sky appreciates a clean, good morning, and the sea's in a good temper sometimes. Don't always think of nature as men and women. If you're kind to nature, nature will understand. These are some of my comforts. You want the earth again. Well, the sea will tell your wish to the clouds, maybe, and perhaps some little drifting cloud will float with the news over to the land, and rest above the cool trees and the yellow gorse and the grass near the chalk pits. So though you can't get the earth again, ma'am, the earth may know. And let's hope she will, and send back her kind regards and very best wishes. Call him again.

ANN. Call him? Why? He won't be far from me.

SCRUBBY. *Call him!*

ANN. Henry! *(A pause.)* Henry! *(Long pause. Rises and goes up centre, exits and returns.)*

[168]

Henry! Henry! Henry! (*Another pause—goes out left and re-enters. At opening left cries out.*) Henry! Henry! (*Pause.*) He must be here. He must be here. (*She dashes on to the deck again. Looks round. Then returning cries once more, wildly, "Henry!" There is no answer. She looks at* SCRUBBY *questioningly.*)

SCRUBBY. He has gone.

ANN (*screams*). Henry!! You haven't looked.

SCRUBBY. U'seless.

ANN. What do you mean? (*Quiet now.*)

SCRUBBY. I know what's happened to him.

ANN. What?

SCRUBBY. *He lives again!*

ANN. Lives! Henry gone back?

SCRUBBY. The dog, ma'am, outside the window. —Perhaps broke through.

ANN. Henry is gone back, alone.

SCRUBBY. The dog, ma'am, outside the window! to resist the fumes, maybe.

ANN. Gone back. I'll follow him.

SCRUBBY. You can't.

[169]

ANN.   Henry wouldn't leave me alone.

SCRUBBY.   He couldn't help himself, madam.

ANN.   But we've been dead a week—

SCRUBBY.   A week! A century! A moment! There's no time here. He's gone back, madam.

ANN.   Then I'll go too.

SCRUBBY.   You can't.

ANN.   I will. I must!

SCRUBBY.   It's impossible.

ANN.   *I will follow.* Henry. Henry. (*Comes down right in front of table, facing front.*)   Henry dear, where are you? It's Ann, dear. Where are you, baby? Just tell me where you are? *Where are you?* I'll come, darling. Just tell me. Henry! Henry!

SCRUBBY.   He won't answer. (*Standing in shadows left.*)

ANN.   Henry. Henry, are you in the flat? I believe you are, Henry; you mustn't be there by yourself—you won't know how to manage anything.

SCRUBBY.   It's useless.

ANN.   I will follow him. I *will*. I will. Henry, listen, Henry. Our love, our great love. (*The*

[170]

drum is heard again.)   It's speaking, Henry, the little wedding ring, that wasn't a wedding ring at all—put it on my finger again.   It's on the mantelpiece.   Henry, don't leave me alone for ever.   It's Ann, your Ann, who wants you.   Henry!   Henry dear!

(*The drum stops.*)

SCRUBBY.   Quiet.   Quiet.   I heard something out there—on the deck.

(*Another pause, then* HENRY *appears in the centre doorway.*)

ANN (*without seeing him, still facing front*). Hello, Henry.

HENRY (*coming down to her partly*).   Hello, Ann.   Quick, dear, be very quick.   There's only a second or two.   I've come to fetch you home, dear. Ready, sweetheart?   (*Holding out his hand.*)

ANN.   Ready, Henry, ready!   (*Turning up and taking his hand.*)

HENRY.   We've such a lot to do, my love.   And such a little time to do it in.   Quick.   Quick.

(*They go out together.   The drum starts again very softly.* SCRUBBY *watches them go.*)

CURTAIN

123